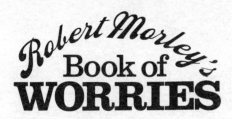

Robert Morley's Book of WORRIES

Robert Morley was born in what is now Julian Bream's house at Semley in Wiltshire in 1908. Originally intended for the diplomatic service, or so he has always told himself, he in fact ended up on the stage where he first appeared as a pirate in *Treasure Island* in 1929. Since that time he has appeared in more than fifty plays, many of them his own, and nearly a hundred films, many of which he cannot remember. The first British actor to play Oscar Wilde on the stage and screen, he is probably best remembered for performances in *The Man Who Came to Dinner*, *Edward My Son*, *Hippo Dancing* and more recently Alan Ayckbourn's *How The Other Half Loves* and Ben Travers' *Banana Ridge*. His most recent stage play is *Picture of Innocence* and on film he was recently to be found in *Someone Is Killing The Great Chefs of Europe*. *Robert Morley's Book of Bricks* is published in Pan.

A regular contributor to *Punch, Playboy* and *The Times Literary Supplement*, Robert Morley lives in Berkshire with his wife and many other relatives.

D1342372

Also by
Robert Morley in Pan Books
Robert Morley's Book of Bricks

Robert Morley's Book of WORRIES

Illustrations by
Geoffrey Dickinson and Michael Heath

Additional anxieties apprehended by
Margaret Morley

Pan Books London and Sydney

The cartoon by Michael Heath on page 19 is reproduced
by kind permission of *Private Eye*

First published in Great Britain 1979 by Weidenfeld & Nicolson Ltd
This edition published 1980 by Pan Books Ltd,
Cavaye Place, London SW10 9PG
© Robert Morley and Margaret Morley 1979
ISBN 0 330 26198 3
Printed and bound in Great Britain by
Hazell Watson & Viney Ltd, Aylesbury, Bucks

*To scrambled eggs on toast
this book is affectionately
dedicated*

Contents

Introduction

'Not to worry then.' 'There's no point in worrying about it. I shall just wait and see.' 'Nothing worries him, that's his trouble.' 'He worries over every little thing, that's what's the matter with him.' 'She can't stop worrying.' 'I'm worried sick.' 'Why worry, it may not happen.' 'What worries me. . . .' Stop there for a moment. What does worry you? That you will miss the boat? That you sense menace in the wind? Not in the wind exactly but here in bed just before the telephone rings. 'What can have happened to the others?'

The purpose of worry, like that of sleep, has never been satisfactorily explained. Are we to identify ourselves as wildlife perpetually threatened, scenting danger but unable to identify the direction from which it may emerge? Does worry prepare the mind for the instant when the decision needs to be arrived at without further delay? Is life a perpetual mock alert? 'When antelopes scatter in all directions when hunted on the plain,' the film commentator claims, 'they are deliberately seeking to confuse the cheetah, to postpone his moment of choice till they are out of his range.'

Having finished the *Book of Worries*, I cannot pretend I am any the wiser as to why I perpetually rush around worrying in all directions.

Carrying the breakfast tray downstairs I am aware of the danger of a sudden fall and of blinding myself on the shattered fragments of the butter dish. The kitchen table achieved, I notice the post lying unopened upon it. 'Who lives in Berkhampstead?' I ask myself, 'friend or creditor?' There is hardly a moment left to celebrate the battle of the stairs before contemplating the terror of insolvency. Do I enjoy frightening myself a dozen times a day? I must do – I have after all been doing so now for seventy years, and in the process I've acquired a certain resilience if not actual courage. There are some worries which have proved enjoyable and others without which life might have been happier, if a lot duller.

When you read that there is another besides yourself who dreads catching a sandal in the jaws of an escalator, who, driving home after an evening on the town, anticipates that just before he gets there he will be intercepted and advised to turn back and not add to the confusion of firemen, who themselves arrived too late upon the scene, or because when I take my seat in the railway carriage I begin to worry lest the train is not the one I intended to catch, or when I am taken to admire a precipice I find myself considering not the view beneath but where exactly I ought to position myself for a final death plunge – will you cease to share my anxieties? Of course not. I do not expect any of you who, like me, dread the thought of falling from a ski-lift or choking to death on a piece of steak to worry any the less just because we have discovered we worry alike. A worry shared is not a worry halved. All men and women share the same, or very nearly the same, imagined worries and a continuing halving of the load could rapidly lead to its disappearance. This would never do for nature's enjoyment or our own. There is happiness, surely, when disaster anticipated is at least postponed. 'How lovely,' we tell ourselves, 'I was convinced I was going to be killed this morning in a fatal crash on the motorway and here I am alive and well and looking forward to the macaroni cheese.'

What, you may ask, is the underlying purpose of this book? To show that all men worry? But all men know that already. To collect all my worries together and arrange them in alphabetical order? What point in that, you ask again. And I must search for another reason for such exhibitionism. To make money? To amuse myself? Both cogent reasons, but neither quite the whole truth. Just as I am wont sometimes to stare in the mirror, distorting my features in an attempt to discover what I shall look like when I have finally gone quite, quite mad, so I have played with worry as a child might take the toys out of the play box and then fail to find room to pack up the whole collection. 'I haven't finished with that one,' I would tell nurse, and the jack-in-the-box for whom I could find no space accompanied me to bed.

If worries are toys, most of which we cannot bear to discard, can we learn to play with them more sensibly? Such discipline is difficult, yet to know when to worry and which one to select can, if learnt, be of enormous advantage. It can even save your life. Driving along the motorway you are worrying lest you may be late for an important luncheon date when the car stalls and you almost but not quite reach the hard shoulder. You then cease to worry about missing luncheon but begin to worry about how long it is going to take to mend the engine and how much it is likely to cost. Suddenly you are catapulted off the shoulder, the car turns over and you fear you may be incinerated in the wreckage. You have stopped worrying about the repairs. You are worrying about facing death. Nothing catches fire but you suddenly become aware that your leg is trapped and you begin to wonder what life will be like without a leg. All previous worries are immediately banished. You recall the legless Douglas Bader and perhaps, because you are growing increasingly light-headed, remember the difficulty he invariably experiences passing the metal checkpoint whenever he needs to go by plane. When the fire engine arrives and you are extricated comparatively intact, you are surprisingly cheerful as they lift you into the ambulance. Saved by the bell or in these days, the siren, you begin to worry about conditions in the casualty ward. What has really saved the day for you is an inherent ability of the worry mechanism to leap-frog the gory details of *ad hoc* surgery by the roadside and in a time of great stress such as this, arrest and reverse the worry load to within bearable limits.

Once he has grasped the concept of the existence of a hidden safety valve, a man can learn to wake himself from a nightmare of anxiety by thinking (as I have trained myself to do) of scrambled eggs on toast, a dish of which I am extremely fond. It is not only the thought of actually eating them, remembering the taste and substance when they are successfully conveyed from pan to buttered slice, but the skill required in the preparation of the dish. There is something about a buttered egg that sustains and fortifies me in my darkest hour and makes me determined that whatever temporary difficulties confront me, I will assuredly taste them again when they are resolved. Hence the dedication of this book.

Author's note: Some of the cross-references in this book are untraceable. This is a conscious effort on my part to increase your worry potential.

Accidents

I need to be in the mood to worry about these. A sudden presentiment, a flash of imagination or indigestion, and out of a clear blue sky a plane falls on the house, or a gust of wind topples a great oak on top of me. Just when things are at their best, a sudden silence occurs and I await the scream from the kitchen as a finger is severed. I imagine the sky suddenly filled with enormous birds that blot out the sun and all life within a ten-mile radius of Reading – hardly an accident, I tell myself, but something for which on certain days I am quite prepared.

I brood frequently on road accidents – those about to happen or those that have already happened. Something tells me that the phone is about to ring and a voice inform me, 'This is the police. We have grave news. . . .'

I am not, I think, accident-prone but others who come to the house manifestly are. 'Mind how you go,' I tell them as they chug out of the gate only to be stranded petrolless a few miles further on their journey. Far worse befalls them than the milk boiling over, but when it does they scald themselves. They fall downstairs, flying glass makes mincemeat of their features, they stand in roads and juggernauts send them hurling into ditches and local cottage hospitals. They fall from a horse and the creature rolls over on to their pelvis; they set their house on fire; they have tendons severed in their legs by housewives pushing baby carriages.

Is it because I seldom get the breakfast, always descend the stairs with exaggerated caution, only walk when I must, never ride horses and only very occasionally do the shopping that I am still unscathed? Do I believe, like Logan Pearsall Smith, that God himself watches over me and, before danger strikes, leans forward from his ineffable seat to bellow, 'Don't touch him, leave him alone, that's my ewe lamb, I tell you'? But if so, how long will the divine protection last or can the Almighty himself be caught napping? If I knew, perhaps I would no longer worry.

But when accidents strike my friends or loved ones, there is surely virtue in keeping calm. 'Nonsense,' I told my son when he once fell on the garden path, 'stop crying, you haven't hurt yourself. You'll be all right in a minute.' It took two nights in hospital and the skill of a plastic surgeon to repair the damage which the stake he had been carrying had inflicted an inch from his jugular vein.

I woke in the dark last night and worried that an accident to an optic nerve had made me totally blind. As dawn gave a glimmer of light, I fell asleep worrying about how to change the ribbon on the typewriter.

Aeroplanes, falling on you

Do you realize that a packet of tissues falling on your head from that height would almost certainly kill you? Paper doesn't normally fall out of planes. What flies off them are things like wings. Remember that the trajectory path is never a plumb-line so keep watching a plane until it is no longer overhead and for some time afterwards. Only then start looking for the next one.

Aeroplanes, flying in

Fear of flying is probably best left to the birds, but even for humans this is a comparatively simple phobia to acquire. Merely repeat to your friends that you are scared every time the thing takes off or prepares to land or while it is poised over Sydenham, and worrying about an intended flight becomes automatic. Days, even months before take-off will pass quickly as you imagine yourself plunging to your doom. You hear the cool, calm voice of the assistant pilot announcing to Air Traffic Control that you are going down – somewhere a priest will be fingering his rosary, two lovers will be entwined, a child held tightly in the arms of the purser – and you face those last few moments when, having removed your shoes, you adopt the foetal position – in so far as your seat-belt permits.

Once you have convinced yourself that disaster is inevitable, you will be in a unique position to interpret the portents connected with your final journey. The flight will almost certainly be delayed while somewhere high up in the administration block an argument is going on. 'Are you saying, Jim, you refuse to fly this kite?' 'I am saying, Major, that until a competent expert has inspected the assistant pilot it would be madness to jeopardize the safety of even the air hostess.' In the end, of course, Captain Jim will be persuaded and, after failing to interpret the announcement coming over the public address system, you will find out somehow that flight z909 to Rome is now boarding at gate twenty. It is then you realize that the gentleman standing behind you in the queue is carrying a bomb. The scenario constructed earlier has become purely academic.

The bomb having been carried aboard safely, you adjust your seat-belt and watch one of the hostesses going through the life-saving drill while you listen to a recording – possibly by David Niven (no one has ever been certain) – which asserts that in the extremely unlikely event of the plane landing on water, it is unwise to inflate your lifebelt before actually encountering the waves. There is also a certain amount of play made with an oxygen mask which, if the captain remembers, will be released in the event of the air pressure coming down along with the plane. When the apparatus is finally clamped over your mouth, you are reminded not to smoke.

While the plane is taxiing for take-off, you will notice some of your fellow passengers listening intently and even glancing out of the portholes as flames burst from the engines. These are spare airline personnel who at least know what the latter ought to sound like. But Jim up there at the controls will have the last word. Roger and out you tell yourself, close your eyes and when you re-open them the ground is out of reach.

Even when you land, your sense of relief is already clouded with the knowledge that you will almost certainly have to fly back one day.

Aeroplanes, meeting loved ones

If you have the flight number of the plane it is possible to check by telephone whether your loved ones are already in the sea or scattered on some isolated mountain top before actually driving to the airport to meet them. If the switchboard operator is as yet unaware of the tragedy or if indeed it has not as yet occurred, you will be told the flight is on time. You will have rehearsed in your mind where you propose to park the car and, if you are an above-average worrier, what you might do if it breaks down on the way to the airport.

Once inside the terminal (sinister word), you will find a board on which all flights but the one you are hoping to meet are listed as delayed or landed. There is no information whatever about your loved ones. You can try asking a bystander or a porter but this is pointless. As you have time to waste, you will find that either they don't know or their interests lie elsewhere. The address system (although far from silent with its repeated request that Mr Slovati travelling from Amsterdam should contact the Information Desk and

'This is your chaplain speaking ...'

that there is a message apparently awaiting Mr Tracy) gives nothing away. Could it be Spencer Tracy? In mounting panic you remind yourself that he is dead and probably by this time so are your relatives. You tell yourself that you too should contact the Information Desk, when suddenly the board is activated and so far as you can judge restates its original position. What was all that about, you ask yourself, and then in a further flurry of excitement you read that your beloved is now on firm ground and if nothing untoward occurs during customs examination will be joining you in about an hour and a half. This is the moment to find something fresh to worry about, like the penalty for smuggling hashish.

Age

On the whole I prefer to worry about other people's rather than my own. As I mature, various problems confront my contemporaries. Mabel, for instance. Should she still be driving? Have I some sort of duty to alert the authorities? It is not so much her eyesight, though heaven knows that is eccentric enough, it's her absent-mindedness. The other day, for instance, when I voiced my terror aloud, she asked which of us was driving. At the speed we were going she ought surely to have known. Then we have the problem of Humphrey, Mabel's husband. It is difficult to estimate his age but whatever it is, he is too old for it. He would be lost without Mabel, yet some instinct for survival now prompts him to walk rather than ride. If they have to go, it would surely be better they went together. Ought I to urge a picnic for them both over Beachy Head?

As a survivor from the life class of 1908, I find myself increasingly questioning other men – never alas women – as to how long they have lived. Why am I now so much more interested in the longevity of homo sapiens? The knowledge thus gained is never entirely satisfactory. An octogenarian brimming with energy serves only to remind me that I would have been wise to have taken some exercise over the years, and to wonder how long it is advantageous for a valetudinarian complaining of a liver well past its prime to tarry.

These are matters merely for passing concern, but I have worried more over the comparative ages of my progeny. I do not mean just that they are younger than myself – I accept the necessity – but that from the moment they arrive there seems to be an inherent time-lag or a sudden acceleration in their development. Surely, I tell myself, that baby is old enough to crawl, this child should not be constantly exploring lavatories, and this grandson – should he be poring over *Playboy* when at his age I was absorbed in Meccano? The days have passed when I used to lie awake fretting about whether my children were sharing an alien couch or the back seat of a car. But I am still as concerned with their comparative age charts as I once was with their school reports. Did I worry lest things might go as wrong for them as they had gone right for me? That they would be unemployed, unmarried, unhappy? Yes I did. Do I still? Certainly. At their age anything could happen to them. At my age what can happen to me?

I read the life expectancy charts and am grateful that by my reckoning I have another fifty years. I am grateful too for an inherent mathematical blockage. No cause for worry here, though others may not be so fortunate. Do men really live to be one hundred and twenty one? In Osaka it's quite common apparently. I come of a long-lived family – aunts toppled over at ninety, uncles collapsed only a few years earlier. Who cares if I worked it out wrong? I have burnt the chart while trying to light the fire. I have burnt my boats too. Others must worry about my age; I have other more pressing anxieties. I shall sit and worry about one of the cats: like me, long past her prime and not a care in the world. She may be pushing fifteen, but what of it? As the vet said only the other day, 'I have a lot of cat patients in their early twenties.'

There are the other and (I like to believe) less selfish age worries. How will they all manage when I am gone? Is there enough life insurance? At least I know the answer to that one. No, and never will be. Shall I worry about being buried alive? That may come later – in the book, I mean. How about if incapacity should render me helpless, incontinent, and a perfect nuisance? I am too heavy to lift, but then again sometimes one wastes away. What excellent worries age affords, but how little time in which to explore them all.

Animals

On the whole I find this is also a worry I would feign leave to others. I have never been able to afford the time or money necessary to join the vast majority of my fellow citizens in their efforts to preserve wildlife. I was born with an inability to agonize about a decrease in the number of tigers alive and well in Sumatra. I have no affinity with big cats and I fear the feeling is mutual. Exploring safari parks in Kenya or on the estates of the nobility I am quite frankly terrified. What I should do if I were to meet a whale I cannot imagine. Sharks keep me from bathing, snakes out of the jungle and once, in the rain forests of the Amazon I turned and ran at the sight of a single ant. I also have a terror of dogs who have not been properly introduced.

I do not wish to be selfish or didactic. I am aware that better men and women than I devote their lives and often their residual estates to improving the lot of beach donkeys and derelict kittens. Others, like Monsieur Cousteau, Mr Attenborough and Mr Scott, demonstrate their concern on television, and who is to say that we or they are poorer for their efforts? I may on occasions go to sleep counting sheep jumping a gate but I am unable to visualize the accidents that must occur to the ones that fail to clear the obstacle.

Some men are cruel to animals and others quite rightly worry that this should be the case. If anyone wishes to share their enthusiasm and compassion I would be the last to discourage them. This book, as I have stated elsewhere, is intended to increase each reader's worry ·

potential. For the inexperienced animal worrier let me counsel that they should at first confine their anxiety to animals and birds kept as pets or beasts of burden. Even experienced worriers find it difficult to concentrate on the species which are good to eat.

Appointments

Like all good worries, this one is usually self-inflicted. However it is even more of an anxiety if someone else has made the appointment for you. Doctor Evans will see you at 12.00. The Board would like to interview you at 10.30. Your bank manager would be obliged if you would drop in this afternoon. From childhood, appointments impinge on happiness. A pre-arranged visit to a dentist prevents an afternoon of pleasure at the ice rink. Later we go to absurd lengths to avoid keeping an appointment. It is impossible to contemplate a successful outcome to any interview. We know already we won't get the job, we will be rejected by the insurance company, our solicitor will advise pleading guilty. As the day on which the appointment has to be kept approaches, panic urges us to cut and run. In whatever role we have cast ourselves, candidate, patient, master of the internal combustion engine, we tell ourselves this is surely not the day to seek a verdict, resolve the issue, decide to throw in our lot with the Uganda Waterworks Board.

Often we are too worried by this time to take positive evasive action. We simply ignore the fact that at five we should be on the corner of the Goldhawk Road to meet our examiner, and instead we go straight home. My goodness, I forgot my driving test, we tell them. How on earth could I have gone and done such a foolish thing? You'll forget your own head next, they tell us. For heaven's sake remember you have an appointment with your chiropodist on Monday.

Where the corn-scrapers' and hair-cutters' appointments are concerned, I have an extremely low worry quotient and quite often manage to keep them. Is it because I am permitted to sit while they stand or crouch? It is the thought of the man behind his own writing desk, or seated at the Board room table or awaiting my arrival with mirror already strapped to his forehead that affrights.

Arithmetic

Less of a worry than it was to children and adults alike thanks to the invention of the computer, it is now, for me at any rate, more of a worry lest the sums are temporarily or permanently in error, in which case man's final calculations may prove as usual to be at fault. I am of a generation most of whom never mastered the art of mental arithmetic and were unable to add and subtract or long divide numbers submitted by keen examiners wishing to test our potential to become actuaries in later life.

For such as I, bank statements, income tax demands and credit card accounts are, when rendered through the post, a worry of such dimensions that we avoid opening the envelopes. Since we cannot add up whatever sums we have spent, there is little point in writing them down. However, some there be who keep careful records, check bills, fill in cheque-book stubs and worry incessantly lest they are overspending. Sometimes in an attempt to clear the decks, I come across my own pocket calculator in some disused drawer and, supposing the battery to be more active than I, spend happy minutes calculating the seconds I have lived or testing the machine's ability to multiply the number nine to the point of infinity – a task of which it usually tires before I do.

Where mental arithmetic is concerned, I like sometimes to set myself simpler tasks: adding up, for instance, the number of people who have accepted my very occasional invitations to a party, realizing I have as usual nowhere to accommodate such a horde and worrying about the alternative arrangements I must make. There are other sums I also fail to do in my head. Once in the dressing-room of Greta Garbo – or what would have been her dressing-room if they had not built a new bungalow for their star – I sat on the lavatory seat of Metro Goldwyn Mayer and worked out how much I must be earning while doing so. If this was not strictly a worry, at least I was bothered by my inability to arrive at a definitive calculation. In bed I sometimes calculate my worth in sterling, adding in round figures the sum I imagine to be at the bank, the money due to me when I have completed my current assignment, the value of the fitments, the going rate of the property, my life assurance were I to die tomorrow, and setting against it my debts to the Inland Revenue and sundry creditors. It is not that I like to worry about insolvency but like most of us I cannot avoid doing so. Besides, there is in my case, thank goodness, a margin for error.

Arrest, wrongful

The fear of wrongful arrest can be happily extended to include shoplifting whenever you pick up an object which is for sale or somebody else's handbag which manifestly isn't; being drunk in charge after just catching the green light; merely standing stock-still in the roadway and shouting 'Bugger Prince Charles' (see Irrational Impulses); every time you use a public lavatory or allow your TV licence to lapse. A case of mistaken identity will cause the doorbell to ring in the early hours and you will be asked to remember what you were doing on any particular date and will subsequently depart for detention at a police station to help the police with their enquiries into a case of multiple rape. The long arm of the law is stretching out in the direction of the watch you bought in Geneva and carried on your wrist through the Green Channel at the Customs a year ago (guilt).

Assault, indecent

Worrying about being charged with indecent assault at the cinema, a worry for which I am indebted to Mr Alan Bennett who owns to this one himself, will help you to take your mind off the film and make you sit so near the screen that you may have cause to worry about eye-strain. You will be on the alert for neighbours of either sex on either side of you. An aisle seat can effectively halve this anxiety, should you wish to do so.

Babies

From the moment they are conceived worrying about babies is quite irresistible. They are guests bidden to a party without signifying the hour they propose to arrive or the shape they will be in when they do. All we know is that once they have condescended to appear they will be in complete charge. It is well to remember that a baby too has initial anxieties. From the moment he opens his eyes he finds himself surrounded by a number of masked strangers, any two of which may be his parents. Life's lottery has commenced. He may not care for the surroundings into which he is so rudely thrust, may wish for peace and quiet after his exertions, not to be passed from hand to hand, hung upside down, weighed, washed and wrapped into a neat parcel, but above all there is the constant worry that some fool may drop him. In this respect I had a particularly nerve-racked infancy – my father always felt a compulsion to hold me above his head and juggle with me.

As I lay in my cot, a week old, my grandmother paid a call, inspected my sister, who had arrived a year earlier, and then me, closed her lorgnettes and remarked, 'The girl is all right, the boy's an idiot.' I may not have heard her at the time but, depend on it, the remark was repeated to me in later months and did little to reassure. As a baby I was a hypochondriac, somewhat overweight, and a nervous traveller envisaging constant collisions with other prams. Kensington Gardens was insanely crowded in those days – the motorway of the park, as we used to call it among ourselves.

Since then, when babies arrive at our house, I try to be asleep, not wishing to add to the confusion. My own children were greeted by me with exaggerated calm and I strove to impart a confidence neither of us shared. Later, of course, I experienced the same foreboding as the average parent does when subjected to sudden cries, moments of utter stillness, unexpected blotches and rashes, small dry coughs, the ability to grasp but not to let go, a reluctance to sit up. Precocity was observed with pride and joy one morning, only to find no sign of it the next – that baby, I would tell myself, used to know where his head was but now he has entirely forgotten. One moment there was the worry lest he was never going to crawl, the next that he had learnt to do so but only into the fireplace. It was not an easy life for either of us. On the other hand when I was a baby I was at least encouraged to put on weight.

Baldness

Years ago this worry was the bane of the orchestra pit. Bald musicians were thought to play more wrong notes than hairy ones and for all we know they may very well do so. Nowadays there are fewer orchestra pits and better artificial thatch but even if you don't play an instrument, growing bald must be a distinct disadvantage unless you are a monk. After all, once your top shows, there is always the suggestion that you may have gone over it. Moreover, there are quite a number of ancillary worries to this problem. Some men buy hats, lose them and have to buy others. Some learn to train their remaining hairs like vines covering a pergola. Others have hair plucked from the nape and sewn into the crown.

Where you wear your hair is important. A man worries when it starts to grow out of his ears and nose, frets when he finds it embedded in the comb. A wig causes others to worry. Can that be his own hair, they ask themselves, and anguish because they cannot be sure. Some men polish their heads until there is a burnished dome reminding us of St Paul's or Telly Savalas.

What is the saddest thing of all things? A woman without love, an angel without wings, or a bald barber peddling hair restorer?

Banks

Most people including myself avoid knowing exactly how much they have in a bank or how large the overdraft. This way they can worry continuously. 'I don't know what my bank manager will say,' they chortle as they sign the cheques. Bank managers, although quite often overdrawn themselves and despite all efforts to make them appear human, are the spectres at the feast to be conjured up at will to fright Macbeth, a necessary fantasy replacement for ogres. An attempt made by the advertisers to hide a bank manager in every cupboard as part of a campaign to convince the public they have little to fear from them was doomed before the presses started to roll. Newspapers recently have been running pictures of a Rolls Royce motor car along with the caption 'Will your bank manager give you a Rolls Royce?' which must prove equally disastrous.

Without the ever-increasing insolvency of their customers, no bank could continue its stately progress along the high streets of Britain, but in order to play their necessary part in sustaining the adrenalin content in their clients' blood, a bank manager may call at times for a reduction of the debt and the interest charged on it. He never seriously envisages anything of the kind actually taking place and it can here be noted that a man or woman maintains roughly the same level of insolvency, allowing of course for inflation, throughout life. There are exceptions to this rule. Sometimes a man will try and find out exactly how much money there is in any one or possibly two banks, he will escalate his liabilities to the three million mark and then either blow his brains out or wisely transfer his remaining assets to his wife and declare himself bankrupt (*see* Bankruptcy). This is what the bank terms 'a bad debt', all others being good ones. Afterwards they may or may not replace one or two of their staff, but usually they soldier on cheerfully enough, philosophically reminding themselves that in the nature of things a bluff must be called once in a while and on this occasion they did actually give their customer a Rolls Royce or quite possibly two.

There are those few who even keep money in their account and sometimes jewellery and the family plate in their bank vaults. A good deal more worry can be generated if this course of action is pursued. Visions of a run on the bank while they themselves are holidaying in Portugal mingle with the lively foreboding that thieves may tunnel in and emerge wearing the family tiara atop their stocking masks. Collapse of the currency, the lowering of the bank rate, the fall of the Dow Jones averages, remind the rest of us that these are the few for whom the financial editors of the daily papers write. We, on the other hand, have nothing to lose but our overdrafts but that, thank goodness, won't stop our worrying either.

Bees

Some people cannot bear to be in the same garden as a bee, so convinced are they that they will become an unwilling partner in the insect's suicide act. A bee sting is more dreaded than that of a wasp

because of the inherent drama involved in the former's kamikaze syndrome when the attack is pressed home. Death could ensue for the attacked and attacker alike. The flit gun and the rolled newspaper are the final solution when all other methods such as covering the jam and removing the cake-stand have failed. Even so, the ultimate destruction of a fellow creature whose dedicated task is the manufacture of honey must be regretted, though at the time a military necessity – and what if the insect escapes and flies off menacingly to call up reinforcements? On the other hand, few people worry about killing a wasp or taking it captive under an upturned tumbler. A wasp when it crosses our path or invades the tea-table is palpably up to no good, whereas a bee searching for its hive or the herbaceous border is plainly confused.

From time to time we read horrific tales of a queen bee exhausted by the mating flight deciding to continue her journey on a passing bicycle while her subjects, determined not to make her feel ridiculous, cling resolutely to the saddle, the handlebars and the rider himself in an endeavour to convince him that from now on he is a living hive. There is little you can do in such circumstances except dismount and await the arrival of a qualified bee-keeper, comforting yourself meanwhile with the thought that bee stings are reputed to be good for rheumatism. Purists might, however, argue that if you already suffer severely from rheumatism you are unlikely to be riding a bicycle.

Birds

Budgies, canaries and mynah birds cause their owners to spend a good deal of time trying to decide what is the matter with them. They are in constant need of birdseed, fresh water, additional mirrors or see-saws, companions, feathers or being spoken to. They must be constantly protected from staying up too late and the cat, and encouraged to venture occasionally outside the cage but rarely outside the house – once is, indeed, usually enough.

Birdlife can become an obsession for those who prefer to watch them in their natural habitat. Men and women pass sleepless hours endeavouring to pinpoint the whereabouts of a crested grebe and are then unable to sleep when they do get to bed because of the hideous doubt that they were once again mistaken in the sighting, and wondering how to retrieve the letter already addressed to Peter Scott.

Taking your own little duck to feed with the others by the pond can be fraught with anxiety lest he tumble in or be savaged by a swan. On the whole it is better, I find, to encourage him to eat the crusts. Birds, as Miss du Maurier observed, can turn nasty. Indeed many hold they are like that already.

Blood Pressure

A lively source of worry and one of many self-generating species. Hence, the more you worry about BP, the more you will have to worry about. There is seldom such a thing as normal blood pressure; it is nearly always too high or too low, like temperature readings. It is a particularly convenient test for doctors because there is no waste material, like blood or urine, to be disposed of and they can spend the time puzzling out what can be the matter with you. Should you interrupt your doctor's bewilderment by speaking, your BP will

bound upwards. Blood pressure is always given as one number over another and in this respect it is as difficult to comprehend or pin down as an income tax form. In general the first number is the diastolic figure, the lower known as the systolic, or just possibly vice versa.

Although remaining the property of the worrier, BP, once established, takes on a separate personality of its own. Certain activities and food are judged bad for it and even casual strangers have to be constantly reminded that the proprietor of a blood pressure does not care to engage in an argument he cannot win, or render a service to others or indeed to himself which involves physical exertion.

In certain department stores shoppers will be confronted with a poster bearing the legend 'Blood Pressure the Silent Killer' and if they have a few moments and a coin of the realm to spare, they may insert the latter into a converted pin-table, enclose their arm in a bandage and wait to read the score displayed in the space where normally you would hope to read 'Free Game'. This is rapidly becoming a new spectator sport and the attendant will write down your score and apprise you of whether or not you have won a visit to your local doctor.

Botulism

My cook book says: 'Clostridium botulinum [is] a germ so deadly that one ounce could theoretically kill one hundred million people. The spores of botulism may resist $212°F$ or boiling temperature, even after several hours of processing, and produce a fatal toxin in the canned product. Botulinus poisoning may be present even if no odour, gas, colour changes or softness in food texture indicate its presence.' The only way to be sure of killing it off, it goes on to say, is by boiling the contents of the tin for fifteen minutes. Now commercial canners are very, very careful – so is the government. About once every thirty years or so one rogue slips through the net, but that doesn't stop every tin in my larder from becoming a potential killer. So all those instructions on the back that say, 'Heat gently. Do not boil or the flavour will be impaired' are ignored. Baked beans have always had an impaired flavour and a certain mushiness which our family, knowing no other, enjoys greatly. This procedure is, however, very difficult to follow with sardines.

Bridges

Suspension bridges cause the most worry. The idea that a journey involves crossing one has been known to reduce the most carefree person to near panic. Is there a route around it? Twenty-five miles is no distance at all if it is possible. Add the likelihood of a windy day and a sixty-mile detour becomes nothing. This worry can usually be attributed to two factors. The first is the look of a suspension bridge – though usually rather beautiful, they don't look safe; there is something unnatural about defying gravity for such a span. The second factor is too many movies of the Tarzan type, where those jungle rope-bridges collapse at the climax, throwing numerous characters into the gorge. Even without hordes of menacing natives, there is just something innately threatening about suspension bridges.

Motorway bridges can be almost as worrying. It is not unknown for snipers to stand on these and take shots at vehicles as they pass underneath. Be on the look-out for this. It is also not unknown for children to throw stones which shatter windscreens or for overhead traffic to collide with barriers, causing the bridge to collapse on top of whoever happens to be underneath. Accomplished worriers should plan their journey accordingly.

In general bridge worry can be taken to an unacceptable point. The protagonist of Albert Camus's *The Fall* has done just this:

'I never cross a bridge at night.... Suppose after all that someone should jump in the water. One of two things – either you follow suit to fish him out and, in cold weather, that's taking a great risk! Or you forsake him there and to suppress a dive sometimes leaves one strangely aching.' Now, to avoid bridges at night because they might be littered with would-be suicides is a rather charming, exotic worry but one that should really be taken up only by those living at least fifty miles from a sizeable river. Otherwise the interference with daily routine is too great to contemplate.

Builders

Supposing they arrive at all – and you will have been able to worry a good deal during the night that in point of fact they will not appear two days running – there will be an early morning realization that you have locked them out and they are ready for coffee. You were hoping they were also ready to continue to knock the walls up or down but the cement mixer is delayed. Building is conducted from headquarters which are constantly out of touch with the battlefield. The general builder only visits the fighting peripherally, usually on the way to a funeral. Most builders moonlight as undertakers or, if you prefer to put it another way, most undertakers moonlight as builders.

However you put it, adding a patio or a swimming pool (see Swimming Pool), installing a damp course on the ground floor or a rumpus room in the roof are opportunities for continuous and prolonged worry for those with hearts stout enough to have accepted the utterly meaningless original estimate. Once battle has commenced the plan of campaign is continually revised, entailing extra time and expense to reach final and partial victory. Indeed only the wealthiest and most determined house-owner demands unconditional surrender and the final terms usually allow for the occupying forces to be withdrawn on the understanding that they will return some day to implement the double glazing or tile the new bathroom walls.

Whereas the professional classes are always reluctant to comment on their previous colleagues' lack of skill when drawing up a will or removing an appendix, a builder, like a hairdresser, habitually expresses contempt for whoever was last on the scene. He is always eager to demonstrate that a sharp blow with a hammer is all that is needed, not only to dislodge the plaster but also to expose the slovenly manner in which the original brickwork was constructed. 'We had better have this one down while we are about it,' he will tell you. 'We don't want it falling down on its own a couple of years from now, do we?' If you demur, you are faced with the problem of how to repair what was originally a slight crack and is now a hideous blemish above the television.

Just as those held hostage tend to grow fond of their gaolers, so

too you will become curiously attached to the invading forces with their perpetual requests for tea, transistors, bathroom and telephone facilities and that you should move your motor car, lend them a step-ladder or find out where the water can be turned off or the electric current disconnected. You will begin to worry about each one of them and ponder how their exceptional personal handicaps, lack of expertise or accident-proneness will enable them to earn a living once they have quit your own premises. Indeed, when the time comes for a final cup of tea and a celebratory cake, you will say goodbye with a measure of regret and to make up for a sense of loneliness may be tempted to invite the neighbours in to inspect the transformation they have wrought on your premises. 'If I may say so without giving offence, old man,' they will tell you, 'don't you feel you've lost something?' 'Upwards of five thousand pounds,' you reply and are left worrying lest you will never be able to afford to pay the bill.

Burglars

Worry is the one thing burglars and their victims have in common. Burglary is a nerve-racking experience for both, the former worrying well in advance of the time set for the excursion. All sorts of things may go wrong. A forced entry may prove impossible, he may set off the burglar alarm or cut his hand on glass. He will worry about the precise moment at which to put a stocking over his head or even that he will forget his tools and to a lesser extent, his sack, although cushion covers are usually available on the premises. If he is able to take on board additional worries along with the silver-plated candlesticks, he may very easily be worrying whether his own premises are being broken into while he has left them unattended.

For the burglar's victims the worries, although equally potent, are somewhat different. Your enthusiastic worrier has probably worried about *his* burglar's possible arrival every day since he brought home his first darts trophy. If he has not already had his home pillaged and sacked, he certainly knows someone who has talked to someone who has a friend who either has experienced the phenomenon himself or lives in a neighbourhood prone to such happenings. Burglar alarms are not very reassuring, since they mostly follow their own devices. There is nearly always one, for instance, ringing in the High Street to which you habitually, like all passers-by, pay no attention. When, however, it rings in your home there are various complicated procedures to follow and if you have not mislaid the instruction book, the police could very possibly arrive within a few hours. The neighbours are almost certainly bound to do so and expect coffee long before that.

Worrying about burglars may even cause you to keep a dog, although the only reliable animal custodian is a goose. Dogs, like burglar alarms, find it hard to recognize intruders, especially as they grow older. They are also, unlike the burglar worrier, heavy sleepers, although they do provide their owners with a number of other worries (*see* Dogs).

As you lie awake in bed puzzling out the sounds you hear in the night caused by the foundations beginning to shift or the water-pipes coping with airlocks, the rape of the dustbin by some suburban fox, or even one of your family raiding the fridge, you will draw the blanket over your head and, once the initial panic has subsided, worry what to do for the best. The chance that this is the big night when your number comes up is statistically remote. There are only on an average 3071 burglaries occurring on any one evening, mostly during the television programmes, and there are some 15,500,000 private houses and an almost equal number of unattended buildings. The odds are, therefore, several tens of million to one that you are the victim. But it can happen. Indeed, as you tell yourself, it is happening at this very moment. What to do? An expert burglar worrier of our acquaintance keeps his clothes on a chair by his bed, has learnt to dress in the dark and then pull over his head one of his wife's stockings. Thus kitted out he descends the stairs quietly but with confidence. He has scared a good many people up to now but never a burglar. In any case the idea is not to scare the latter, merely to point out that he was the first on the scene and must ask the intruder to retire from the contest or at worst halve the booty.

On the whole, although worrying about stockinged faces peering through bedroom doors and men or even women in balaclava helmets armed with staves demanding the keys of the safe is inevitable, it cannot be included in my list of recommendations. When it occurs, I recommend a deliberate de-escalation of panic. Tell yourself that though you may have lost one golf trophy, you might easily win another if only you could find out what is the matter with your swing, get out of bed and practise a little with the poker you have brought upstairs with you for another emergency, put the keys of the safe outside the door, and go back to bed and try to get some sleep.

Burial, alive

The fear of being buried alive is fairly general. Few people travel for very long in tunnels or explore underground cities in Anatolia without savouring occasional thoughts of substances caving in on them and experiencing an acute sense of relief when emerging into fresh air (see Pollution). However, it is also possible to worry about being lowered into the ground when others imagine, wrongly, that your life is over.

If you should wake up after a time and be faced with the task of lifting your own coffin lid, there is obviously going to be a major worry as to whether such activity will result in your eventual release. Decapitation, excision of vital organs, extensive blood-letting and even dismembering have at times been suggested, and presumably acted upon, as ways to avoid such a contretemps. The reader may now wish to reconsider the actual arrangements for his own funeral.

Burial, dead

Children usually do not have a dread of being buried alive or, if they do, they mercifully keep it to themselves. However, they usually insist at some stage of their lives on burying something themselves, a loved pet or the already decaying corpse of a hedgehog or a crow. It is usually only in later life they start giving serious thought as to how their own remains should be disposed of, how many to invite to the funeral, who is to conduct the service and which graveyard to select. Usually, in the more picturesque churchyard, the prime sites have already gone and any worry that the deceased-to-be experiences on realizing he has left the whole thing altogether too late, he may wish to transfer to his surviving relatives on the day by leaving instructions for them to put him into the herbaceous border or under the hammock. This is never easy to arrange and even if he only stipulates that his ashes are to be scattered on the local cricket pitch, his loved ones may encounter difficulties with the groundsman. Nor is it always advisable to leave the final disposition to others, unless you feel they are not likely to have enough to worry about when death occurs. Ashes do not always scatter as one would wish them to do, nor is it advisable to leave them lying about in urns or, as one widow of my acquaintance did recently, have them immolated in an egg-timer, unless you like really hard-boiled eggs.

A good deal of thought and worry can go into planning your own burial service and a corresponding amount of worry on the probable cost and the likelihood of your wishes being observed. How can you be sure that your heirs won't ignore the codicil stipulating that only the best champagne shall be drunk and the pallbearers be suitably rewarded with plum cake? Then again, exactly how many can you count on turning up? You don't want the place half-filled – better perhaps to stipulate funeral private, thus ensuring that no one will remark on the little interest the event arouses.

Only the bravest will let the possibility of a memorial service pass unchallenged. Better to nip the idea firmly in the bud with a codicil. Attendances are at the best uncertain, and if one has reached a respectable age, it is useless to expect one's contemporaries to risk turning out in fog or a snowstorm. Leave services of thanksgiving, as they are ambiguously titled nowadays, to my profession. We adore them.

Cancer

Almost certainly this is the first worry you turn to when sampling these pages. Cancer worry is like the late Henry Irving: in a class by itself. It takes precedence over approaching blindness or loss of hearing, personal failure of any kind, the weather and the life hereafter.

There is something seriously wrong with you if you do not imagine you have cancer at least once a month. There will be subsequent short periods when the spot having disappeared, the lump having subsided, the cough become quiescent, the voice mysteriously regaining its timbre, you will tell yourself it was after all one more false alarm. But soon the bell will be ringing again in your ear. Stepping off the bathroom scales you will appear at the breakfast table in sombre mood. 'I have lost,' you tell your wife, 'three pounds.' 'Well done,' she says, as you open but do not read the morning paper, your thoughts on other things than the state of the Coal Board. You are wondering about life assurance. 'I hope,' you may remark with as much sang-froid as you can muster with your mouth full of toast, 'I haven't got cancer.' There, it's out. But your little bombshell makes no serious impact. 'Very unlikely dear, you don't look like a cancer sufferer to me,' your wife replies. But

45

even supposing you did, no one would want to tell you at this stage. There is nothing for it but to carry on the daily round but with a new perspective brought by the changed situation in which you now find yourself.

On the way to the station you will for once not worry about missing the train. There will be others you can catch – not as many as you had supposed last night perhaps but plenty nonetheless. After all, a man does not lose three pounds in ... you are not quite sure when you last weighed yourself but it cannot have been all that long ago. A man doesn't lose three pounds period. A fellow commuter is by your side. 'Good morning, what a lovely morning.' 'It is indeed,' you tell him, 'we are lucky.' You are determined to give him no hint of the inevitable catastrophy which confronts you. While he is giving you his opinion on the present predicament confronting the Prime Minister, you are assessing him as a possible pallbearer and then reminding yourself that these things are best left to professionals.

The office or the factory gained, the worry will recede for lengthy periods of enforced activity, although your secretary or the foreman may occasionally find you, energies arrested, staring thoughtfully into the distance. Exactly how many aspirins are needed for the fatal dose? Accuracy is important. Too many aspirins apparently simply don't work – you may wonder why, but must accept the fact. Then again, what about a quiet swim off the Monte Carlo rubber beach, leaving your clothes neatly packaged with the dressing-room attendant and a letter of farewell in the pocket of your blazer? The problem here is that the presumption of death will complicate life for your heirs in the event you are not washed up speedily off the Croisette. Ought you to find out about the tides? Then again, the French would probably not bother to search. If you waited till summer the water might just be possible off Sidmouth. On the other hand a final evening at the casino might be pleasurable. You could always post the winnings home.

There are so many matters to be viewed from your new perspective you will be pleasurably surprised to discover what a fine person you have turned out to be, almost all sense of self-pity banished by consideration for others. Would the family wish to say goodbye and how should you conduct death-bed interviews, supposing you don't go abroad for your final holiday? What about the funeral (*see* Burial), and the announcement in the papers? There is surely scope here for grateful thanks.

By evening you feel surprisingly relaxed and are asleep as soon as your head touches the pillow. You wake and suddenly remember how little time is left. The bathroom scales may tell you exactly how long. You have gained five pounds. There is nothing the matter with you, until next time of course. There is, however, something seriously wrong with the bathroom scales.

Cars

An enormously productive worry, basically of three kinds. Will it start? Will it stop? What is happening to it when it is stationary?

A whole scenario can be created should the first fail to happen. There is no way of getting to the office, the shops, or taking the children to school. There are so many conditions in which the internal combustion engine can fail to combust – lack of petrol, rising or falling damp, sparkless plugs, battery failure, the unknown factor – and in the early stages of car sickness, by which we do not mean passenger sickness (*see* Children Sick on Journeys), motorists tend to ignore the symptoms. They prefer to keep a separate personal worry tank and take no firm action until, when the exhaust falls off, they are able to transfer the lot to a capable mechanic and then worry about whether he is capable – or honest.

Very few cars enjoy even moderately good health, and driving one is like nursing an invalid who only very occasionally rallies from a fatal illness. Every day your car is losing strength and value unless you can nurse it successfully for many years, after which it takes on, like a nonagenarian, a sort of spurious value to yourself and others.

Sooner than you thought it needs expert geriatric care, often major surgery. Besides listening to the throb of its heartbeats, the state of its kidneys, the condition of its reflexes, the driver is watching the other patients in the crowded wards of our motorways, observing their various symptoms, their irregular gaits, their demeanour, their painful lack of co-ordination. He must be prepared not only for those so weak and enfeebled as to bar his passage but others of such unstable behaviour as to involve his own patient in imminent assault. Often when assaults occur further down the endless corridor, he will be forced temporarily to disconnect the intensive care apparatus attached to his own charge and wait impatiently while strangers a mile or two ahead are separated and towed away by emergency teams to the car hospital or merely left, all life now extinct, on the hard shoulder. Small wonder then that when the whole ghastly business has to be repeated on the evening round, he is eager to park the patient in the carport, gargle with whisky to get the stench of ether from his nostrils, and omits to tell his wife that the invalid shows every sign of developing a bedsore or, as it is called in motoring circles, a flat tyre. Besides, hopefully there are other things to worry about, like the lawn.

When your car is involuntarily halted, so many worries will suggest themselves, from fear the engine will begin to boil to what happens if you miss the 5.30 to Budapest, that it would be impossible to list them under this heading. On these occasions one idea leads to another with increasing and pleasurable intensity. A lingering doubt that you killed that cat passing through Godalming will expand from theorizing that a slightly more violent swerve might have killed you to the fate of the Duke of Edinburgh's more or less perpetual appeal on behalf of other cats – Bengal tigers.

No less a worry may be caused by what for some reason is referred to in motoring circles as parking. Even if you find somewhere to leave the car, most motorists don't know how to park, which worries some but by no means all of them. There is even a minority of those at the wheel who are not too distressed if they scratch wings and bumpers, particularly other people's. Most are moderately skilled at reversing into a prescribed, but seldom accurately judged, space. On the other hand many are unable to halt their vehicles unless proceeding forward at the time. This enormously increases not only the worry load but the distance they will have to separate themselves from the appointed rendezvous. However, once a position is secured the driver will alight and walk away, worrying about whether he is sufficiently close to the kerb to avoid further trouble. He will also worry about the number of yellow lines on which the vehicle is now standing and the location of the local car pound. He will also try to remember whether he locked the car door and boot. Some motorists prefer to leave their vehicles off the street altogether, in which case they will be worrying on which floor of the multi-storey car park they finally decided to leave their charge and what parts of the whole are likely to be removed or exchanged while they are elsewhere.

Sometimes a time factor connected with meters is involved, in which case worry increases with every second registered on wrist watch or half-hunter. On the walk or often the run back to his beloved, worry will reach a climax. Indeed, retrieving a vehicle is a climactic experience, often only equalled by that experienced on the

drive home when the full horror of what might have been happening there gradually mounts (*see* Absence from Loved Ones). In the unlikely event of the car having been recovered intact, the worry cycle rotates of its own accord to register possible failure to start on the dial of anxiety.

Asking the way is another horrendous worry for those who do not care overtly for contact with their fellow men, and is often postponed until you are at least one hour late for luncheon. A lengthy interrogation of the deaf, feeble-minded and other variously handicapped citizens to ascertain the exact location of Seymour Road will fuel your panic tank and tempt you to abandon the whole venture.

I recommend addressing your enquiries to men and women whom you have caused to dismount from their bicycles, which seems to have the effect, often but by no means always, of concentrating their minds on your problem. Once they have removed their machines and themselves to a place of safety on the pavement, you will be informed that you are at present headed in the wrong direction. Turning your vehicle round is out of the question, and you must first be prepared to face a maze of one-way streets at the centre of which stands the town hall or the post office, both, alas, unidentifiable when you encounter them.

The courage which comes of despair will now enable you to halt the traffic behind, ignore the hoots and accost a traffic warden, who approaches with the customary literature to affix to your windscreen. 'I am not parking,' you explain, 'just looking for Seymour Road.' Traffic wardens baulked of their prey in this manner are surprisingly co-operative, enjoying the disarray you are causing their natural enemies behind you. 'If you go straight on to the second lights and turn left you are in George Street. Then if you go on till you come to a roundabout and then go left, you can take the underpass and that brings you out on the Anlaby Road. After that your best plan is to ask again.' The next time you stop, you are not only not in the Anlaby Road but among a small crowd of would-be bus passengers eager to encourage you to be on your way and not loiter by the stop sign. Unless you intend to drive round and round until tea time, you should now concentrate either on finding a phone box in working order (*see* Phone Box) so that you can ring your host and demand he set out to find you, or search for an Indian cyclist, preferably wearing a turban. Sikhs are expert trackers and if you can teach yourself to listen to their directions and not be distracted by the problem he must face after washing his hair, you may, if you have a good memory, eventually reach your journey's end.

Cats

Feline animals are mysterious and seemingly very independent. They come and go as they choose and disdain company they haven't selected. This does not stop the cat owner from worrying. The first worry is choosing the animal – pedigree at a great sum or moggy from the card in the post office? However, many cats come unbidden. One cat arrived at our house on Christmas Eve, and having gained entry what with the spirit of the season, goodwill and all that, she almost immediately produced seven kittens. Then there was the worry of finding homes for the offspring. This is easily solved. Give them to friends of the children, who will go home and successfully beg, 'Please, can I keep it?' The kitten then proceeds to choose it's favourite bit of furniture to sharpen its claws on. It won't do any harm – no, not yet, but as the cat grows, the furniture diminishes. Then the cat takes to wandering about the neighbourhood. Where is it? Is it safe? Have you taught it proper road sense? Or is it terrorizing the lady next door who has a thing about cats? A black cat I once had, a huge, long-haired animal, took to leaping onto my neighbour's roof, gaining entrance through the window to the master bedroom and then, perched on the bedside table, staring at the lady of the house until the intensity of the gaze woke her up. Both found the experience unnerving.

The cat, having trained the owner to produce at least two good meals a day, at some point goes on hunger strike. No more will it eat any of the variety of tins produced by manufacturers who know what is good for cats. No, it rejects them all, and watches with pleasure while the worrying mistress cooks up liver, fish, roast chicken – all under the slightly mocking eyes of the cat, who sniffs, mews and rejects speciality after speciality, preferring now and then to catch its own meal. One more worry. What to do with the variety of small creatures brought into the house in varying states of health or death? But the real, underlying worry of every cat owner is a simple and basic one – 'Does that furry, superior creature like me?' That is impossible to resolve.

Children

All parents demand of their children that they should be permitted to worry about them. Our innermost doubts and anxieties lest our offspring are not of the stuff senior oil executives and lady newscasters are made of we keep to ourselves. All I want is that my child should be happy, we tell chance acquaintances, seeking to enquire why our son has left the firm of chartered accountants he joined so gleefully when he came down from university and is now driving a mini-bus load of drop-outs and possibly drug smugglers across Cappodocea.

One daughter is studying to become a hospital almoner; the other has shacked up with a property developer in Milton Keynes, who is already married with a young family he does not propose to abandon. You cannot see much future for either of them, but it is possibly the white sheep you worry about more than the black. You cannot tell your daughter already steeped in care for others that you would be happier if she could meet a fellow she fancies and, even more important, fancies her, any more than you can persuade the other that what worries you about Ferdinand is not his Afro-style haircut and the single ear-ring – heaven knows you are no racist – but that, in case he suddenly decides to return to Nigeria, she should at all costs try to avoid pregnancy. There is no doubt in your mind that she has recently put on a bit of weight.

Readers may think I prefer not to dwell on the worries associated with children during their childhood. The reason is partly that such worries are numerous enough to take up the whole book and partly because all the myriad of disasters I envisaged for my own children in comparatively early life, such as contact with runaway juggernauts, rabid squirrels or molesting adults, were by some miracle successfully bypassed. It is now the sudden absence of a grandchild from the house which causes me to walk briskly towards the sheeted swimming pool lest he be using it as a trampoline. His parents are spread across the sitting-room floor along with the Sunday supplements. There is no longer danger from that quarter in any case – they have learnt to swim.

Cholesterol

This substance might have been invented with a worrier in mind. It is actually a white, waxy-looking crystalline alcohol present in human tissues, but to most people it is butter and eggs. It also has a wonderful duality in that it is definable but fairly immeasurable for the lay person. Also the professionals seem happily divided over how good or bad it is. The worrier can spend hours charting his cholesterol intake, then when bored by that, he can go to a library and find a nutrition expert who feels that humans should only ingest products high in cholesterol, thus freeing himself for other worries.

Christmas

Before Christmas the anticipation of and the actual arrival of carol singers on the doorstep is, next to wrapping-paper and cellophane, the first anxiety of Christmas for most people. The very notion of a band of strangers or, what is worse, neighbours pretending to be wandering minstrels and beseeching alms after completing a ragged verse or two of 'Good King Wenceslas' is one no householder can take in his stride. Dare one cut them off almost at the start of the concert by flinging open the front door and calling out, 'Happy Christmas. Anyone for Coke or sherry?' Possibly the best course is to leave the front door ajar and try to give the impression that there is nothing you and your cat enjoy more than your house cooling down while you listen to the Christmas sound borne on the frosty night air.

Then, there is the problem of how much to give and above all when. There are two schools of worry on this matter. A fiver handed over immediately with a word of heartfelt appreciation and the wish that none should catch cold on your account will speed them firmly on their way, and will ensure your being able to watch what is left of 'Mastermind' on the box. But they are sure to be back next year and possibly some of the bolder spirits even before then. The alternative is to exhaust their repertoire and then challenge them to sing an old Creole slave carol – 'The Lord told the ox not to eat at the manger, to keep the stall warm and wait for the stranger'. Then express disappointment at their inability to do so while tendering a small coin, making sure you yourself insert it in the box provided, which you inspect to see if it is a charity registered under the official Act of Parliament. It may well be you will be left in peace for some Christmases to come.

Apart from the carol singers, you will be worrying about where to spend Christmas. Whatever you decide, you will worry.

'Would you mind very much if Alan and I didn't come this year, Mother? It's just we thought it might be nice to be in our own home for once. I know that, darling, but last year we had to go to Alan's parents and next year we'll be coming to you. If you'll have us, of course. Father seemed perfectly well when we were there last month. If he is going to be ill, I'm sure he doesn't want all the bother of people milling around. There are four of us now and the baby is teething and you know how he feels about children screaming. I'm telling you, darling, they will be screaming. Mother, they won't stop suddenly just because it's Christmas. Juliet always screams more at Christmas, she gets so excited. Well, darling, of course they love their Grannie, but I must say I've never noticed that. If you think they are unmanageable, surely that is all the more reason to keep them at home. You can still go to Midnight Mass. You can get a taxi, Mother, as long as you order it well in advance. We will ring up, I promise, just after the Queen's Speech. No, you don't have to book it. I shall just dial. It's different with STD. That's ridiculous, Mother. I shall send you a turkey and then you will have to cook it, otherwise it will go bad. Very well then, I'll send you a cooked turkey. You always used to say you preferred cold turkey. Splendid, we'll have them next time we stay. There is no rule that says you have to pull crackers at Christmas. You can pull crackers any time as long as you keep them in a dry place.

'Our presents? How about posting those? Not if you wrap them up properly. You know how good you are with parcels. George is going on rather about a hamster. No, Mother, no one is expecting you to do that. You can send George the money and he'll go to a pet shop and buy one. I will find out for you and let you know. I imagine about a pound. That's very generous of you darling. He can spend the rest of it on a cage with one of those treadmills. You haven't had any Christmas cards? Mother, it is still October. The Post Office always say that in the end they have hundreds of postmen sitting round thinking the sorting machines must have broken down. Mrs Turnbull says what? Mother, why should there be a milk strike? Who does she think are going on strike? Mother, the cows can't go on strike. It's very painful for them to be on strike. Nothing is happening to the world, Mother, there are exactly sixty-two shopping days to Christmas and they are all going to be hell.'

After Christmas 'Darling, just rang up to say thank you for the lovely present. Know I should be writing but sure you'll forgive this once. We got your letter. Oh, I'm so glad. We thought it might be useful by the telephone. I'm sorry darling, I *meant* in the loo. For an idiotic moment I thought we'd sent you something else. But your present to us is simply divine. Much too good to use every day. I shall keep it for special occasions. I've never had one before, not that kind anyway. Where on earth did you find it? Harrods, ah! You're so marvellous with presents. I wish I had your gift. Of course I don't want to change it. Which department did you find it in at Harrods? It's so vast, I was thinking about giving some as presents myself next year. The garden equipment department. I didn't expect anywhere, only sometimes Harrods move things around at Christmas. I thought it might be in presents or hall of tomorrow. The garden department ... hold on one moment. I just have to let in the cat. Darling, are you still there? George says thank you too and we are going to plant them in a special border right under the dining-room so we shall be able to smell them at breakfast. I am talking about the seeds you sent us in that divine container. I shall plant them myself as soon as my hand is better. I burnt it. Some fool sent me oven gloves which weren't fireproof. I don't know why people don't try out that sort of thing themselves first. Bloody lunatics. I've a good mind to sue, only I've lost her bloody card. Thank God at least I won't have to bother to thank her.'

Clothes

This worry is much more fairly shared these days between the sexes.
The time when men strived for conformity and women to look different has now passed. If a man decides to wear a safety-pin attached
to his ear, he may worry before he arrives at the gig lest others should
be sporting theirs. No woman spending the night at Windsor Castle

would deliberately choose to wear the identical dress chosen by the sovereign; even at Royal Ascot contingency plans must be formulated and a variety of hats carried in the car boot. The Ascot authorities consider that gentlemen frequenting the Royal Enclosure will have enough to worry about trying to find a winner and for this one occasion try to remove any extraneous anxiety about dress with the exception of the cost of hiring the required outfit.

On all other occasions it is now customary for the male rather than the female to display. The stuffed shirt has disappeared, along with the black tie. The frilled front and the coloured bootlace may now adorn the breast. It cannot be long before the codpiece is once again obligatory wear on the outside rather than the inside of the pants.

Women tend to worry more about what they should wear at dusk than at dawn: it is sufficient to go to work in a pair of sensible slacks and a duffle coat and to rely on the disparity of the slogans emblazoned on the tee-shirt beneath. At night the perpetual chant that she has nothing to wear seldom serves as an excuse for complete nudity.

What one wears has increasingly become a statement of image – jeans, caftans, polo-necks, the little black dress, proclaim and establish the identity of the wearer. As few have clearly defined their identity (or if they have found one are never sure if anyone else will find it acceptable) dressing for any occasion becomes a pleasurable agony of indecision. More and more people are now content to whittle their wardrobe down to two or three items and become known as the woman who always wears that bathrobe thing, or the man in the pinstripe blazer with the white flannel breeches and riding boots.

Few men today care or even dare to sport the conventional three-piece. We may be en route for the office but fashion demands we are off salmon fishing or contemplating a day devoted to furniture removing. Whatever costume we affect must carry a hint of menace. Rape or armed robbery is afoot – our umbrella telescopes into a cosh, our handbag may or may not lawfully belong. Trilbys are out, balaclavas in. We may carry a season ticket for the Morden line but our destination is almost certainly Everest – hence the fur-lined jacket and the climbing boots.

Women dress to stay in the game, men to stop playing it. Both worry lest appearance deceives.

Colds

Highly recommended as a worry filler when there is nothing much about. Like all the best worries, this one is capable of great expansion. Besides worrying about taking to your bed and really enjoying lightly poached eggs and medicinal claret on a tray, you can review all, or very nearly all, future engagements, some of which you are looking forward to but most you are dreading. You may have to miss 'Hiawatha' at the Albert Hall, but you certainly can't go to tea with Mildred's mother and admire Mildred. It simply isn't fair to give colds to babies. You must postpone visiting the sick and the partially deaf – colds cause further complications here. Then, of course, you might have to spoil yourself afterwards with a week in Paris and you can begin worrying about that. It is good to plan for your convalescence but do not forget to worry about the dangerous complications a cold can bring. My colds always go to my chest, alas, and a contingency plan about hospital or private nursing home admission is only common sense.

Precautions against catching colds from others often entail my discouraging suffering acquaintances from approaching too near, and may motivate my continuing worry about increasing deafness. The theory that nothing cures a cold quicker than sexual activity may cause further worries on this splendid worry subject.

Conservation

A most useful all-purpose worry, the vigorous pursuit of which will find you many new friends and could lead to some interesting journeys. If there are only twenty-seven deep-throated Mackenzie Prairie Dogs extant in Peru, you might want to say a fond farewell to them. Men like the Duke of Edinburgh and Peter Scott worry a great deal about conservation, as did Prince Bernhard before he met with his accident. They appear younger than ever in recent photographs.

Once you are prepared to worry seriously about the extinction of species, destruction of crumbling cottages, extension of motorways, proliferation of electric light cables and the proposed pulling down of Buckingham Palace, you will have joined Sir John Betjeman and Spike Milligan at the committee table. At night you can lie in the dark worrying about crayfish and conserving the earth's natural resources. Or you may care to concentrate on how the grandchildren will manage in a world depopulated of praying mantis.

Once you realize everything is threatened, including eventually Marks and Spencers, you will find anxiety spread so thin it is hardly noticeable. In the process you will acquire so many badges and stickers for your motor car that it will be a very real worry where to put them. You may even tell others that with so much disappearing so rapidly, you simply haven't time to worry about yourself. This will not be true. For one thing, you will worry you are not rich enough to be both a friend of Holland Park tube station and a life president of the Tenterden to Rolvenden railway. For another, sheer physical exhaustion from cleaning the Grand Union Canal in the morning and playing your full part in forming a living chain of protest across the Watford bypass in the afternoon will make you aware that you should have put on a dry pair of socks at lunchtime and you may be in for a severe cold (*see* Colds).

Constipation

Ever since we were taught to write our name in the school register each morning after bowel evacuation, this has been the most absorbing anxiety. Nowadays it is enormously helped by advertisements for laxatives and other aids to what is euphemistically referred to as 'regularity'. Not to be a regular guy in this context means we are depicted with a habitually sullen expression before discovering the delights of All Bran or Kruschev Salts and in days gone by, alas, we actually leapt over a gate once we had mastered the routine of the daily dose. This is one of our rare zero-rated worries, and when removed by a successful visit to the water-closet, it produces a short period of exhilaration and even, after a brief glance over the shoulder to reassure there is no blood in the stool, a search for available gates over which to vault in triumph. But so absorbing does the habit of bowel worry become, especially in later years, that it will not be long before doubt about tomorrow's performance sets in.

The cultivation of bowelitis, as this worry is commonly referred to in medical circles, has on the whole little to recommend it unless you happen to be in the business of colonic irrigation or pharmaceutical manufacture or sales. Moreover, it often manifests itself immediately after breakfast, a time when your worry potential should be at its peak and be capable of infinite diversification. To avoid clogging the worry pores along with the colon, it is wise to seek out the doctor's consulting room and hand this one over to him. With the advance of medical knowledge, this will prove for him only a slight worry, unless he happens to be severely constipated himself.

Coughs

These are symptoms, not diseases. Take them to your doctor and he can give you something serious to worry about.

Death Duties

This enormously rewarding worry is reserved for the wealthy, alas. The presumption that it is one of the few worries man can carry beyond the grave is not as yet substantiated and it is difficult for all but a very few readers to understand such altruism. Often worry will lead to action and the owner of a pleasant estate in Somerset will find himself early in middle age bidding farewell to his gardener and departing for Jersey, the Isle of Man or Bogota, where he will live in terror that death will come before sufficient time has elapsed for the purpose of the original manoeuvre to become viable or that the government during the doldrums of a Friday morning sitting may pass a Bill rendering the whole expedition pointless.

He will also, of course, worry about how much more expensive tax consultants are to maintain than outdoor staff, whether his heir fully appreciates the sacrifice he has made and will continue the monthly cheques, how he can nip back home again for the Test Matches, why he has no friends on Jersey or the Isle of Man and, if he has chosen the latter, what the hell to do about the noise of motor cycles (*see* Money).

Dieting, health

This is a worry I can share with my friends, particularly if they are planning to invite me to dinner. 'Just a simple green salad, no dressing, bit of a small orange if you have one and oh, yes, I'm allowed onion yoghurt.' Where they are to find onion yoghurt is for them probably worry number one. It may take them a day or two, and then there's the worry of when to serve it to me. The other guests are having melon and prosciutto, Peking Duck with seaweed and pancakes, and chocolate soufflé. Too early and I will have finished before they are into the melon, too late and my wistful, dog-like expression will spoil their enjoyment or I may wolf the seaweed.

The object of a diet is usually connected with other anxieties (see Weight, Gall Bladder, Love Life, Diabetes, Anorexia) but is more often brought on by wardrobe shrinkages. A dress or suit which fitted perfectly last summer is now unwearable, thanks to the extraordinary treatment it has received at the dry-cleaners. Worry about when to start, what to give up and when to stop will pleasantly employ waking hours. A measure of success may temporarily be achieved and the coat buttons or the skirt zips will do up in another week. But then the inevitable occurs – the chocolate is bought and munched surreptitiously, the muffin accepted and buttered, and the realization that you have a serious character defect provokes another worry. Why cannot I give up éclairs? There is some craving here you cannot rationalize. You eat (you have read somewhere) to compensate – but for what? Hunger? That is too easy an answer, and like me, you will begin to worry about being rejected as you bite the wafer around your ice cream cone.

Health Diets. Everyone ingests a daily ration of poison. How to cut down the dose? This excellent worry involves a good deal of physical exercise in the pursuit of trouble-free bran and cabbages reared in natural surroundings. Because the premises where these can be obtained are usually separated from the desk or counter, and each other, by considerable distances, worry can be enjoyed in anticipating not being able to reach them in your lunch hour and whether they will be open after 5.30 p.m. There is also the worry of how molasses, living Korean yeast and pine needles can be consumed at other people's boards. 'Would you mind if I came half an hour earlier and borrowed your mix-master?' Living on asses' milk and honey gathered from wild bees may eventually produce a state of complete physical perfection, but long before that state is reached, you will be worrying about how few people there will be to notice (*see* Loneliness).

Aphrodisiac Diet. You will worry about the expense of this one and how long you should wait before putting it to the test.

Health Farm Diets. I find this a most pleasurable form of worry, capable of infinite expansion, as I undergo the preliminary check-up and subsequent treatments. Health farming, like all agricultural enterprises, is designed to make a profit for the farmer and, like me, you will be able to worry a good deal about the cost. (How can such charges be justified for half a grapefruit, forty-five minutes daily hell with a Japanese masseur and a shared hot pool?) After a fortnight we shall return to normal service – expense account luncheons and take-away Chinese – and to our normal weight, and can start worrying about whether we can afford another spring-cleaning next year.

Dogs

For many of us, particularly myself, a dog is a set of sharp teeth mounted on four legs. To see one approaching, even on a lead, automatically activates a whole sequence of worries. Most important, is the owner strong enough to restrain the brute? Large dogs will almost certainly attack our throats, smaller breeds our legs or ankles. This calculation is complicated by the creature's ability to jump. Although in theory a dog is only allowed one bite, he is allowed apparently any number of sniffs, barks and growls. A dog doesn't have to be reminded of these privileges but his owner usually believes he would like to be.

'Good dog,' they will tell him, or, 'That's a good boy then', and many will even invite you to extend a hand to be smelt and licked by the brute. 'He just wants to get to know you,' they will say. It doesn't occur to them, as it has already done to you, that an average dog is pretty catholic in his choice of matter to sniff and lick, and seldom washes his nose. Besides, you have a slight cut on your finger. Dogs' noses are supposed to be cool and damp and you will need your handkerchief once the inspection is over. On the other hand, if the nose is dry, he may be sickening for something, quite possibly rabies.

It is well known that if you are afraid of a dog he can sniff your terror. Should you encounter him unleashed and walking on his own like yourself, it is unwise to suddenly cross the road – you may get knocked down – but if you don't, the dog will almost certainly follow you and attempt to verify his suspicion.

Owning a Dog. Next to being frightened of them, owning one provides a fruitful orchard of worries. There is always the thought of losing him and of his subsequent fate, that he may be involved in a fatal skirmish with another dog or a moving vehicle, that he will learn to worry sheep or postmen and have to be put down or has been already. The love life of their pet causes owners to worry constantly. Marriage, unless consumated by the stud book, is frowned

upon for bitches. There is no movement as yet for bitches lib, and they are frequently imprisoned during their even more frequent mating seasons. But sooner or later they inevitably escape to bring disgrace and unmarried motherhood into their owner's life. Then there is the worry of what to do with the first generation and, if you don't get the mother seen to, with the second, third and fourth.

Obedience Test. Although they will worry about this for some time, most dog owners will at length be able to teach themselves to obey their dog.

Guard Dogs. The unacceptable face of capitalism separated from you by wire netting which is bound to give way one of these days. Hurry past.

Crufts. Unlike the Miss World contest, this is open to both sexes. Chaperones worry about practically everything. If the contestants worry, there is no telling. The winner last year was reported unhappy because Yorkshire Terriers are discouraged from becoming guide dogs.

Eggs

Here we come to a classic worry. This is a universal problem which can be turned over in the mind endlessly, each time approaching it from a different angle – biblical, historical, scientific, philosophical – oh, it is a delight in its complexity. Consider: which came first, the chicken or the egg? Mankind has been worrying about this for centuries (along with the problem of whether Adam had a navel and how many angels can fit on the head of a pin) and come to no conclusions. Isn't it wonderful? At the same time it is simple and infinite. It has the added advantages of being personally inconsequential and completely insoluble. Or is it? It is a perfect worry in that it can be returned to with regularity and enthusiasm.

The egg, of course, produces more mundane worries, such as, if you have hens, will they lay any? Or, if you are balancing the week's shopping in a basket far too small, will they break? Should we really eat seagulls' eggs and, come to think of it, what about that spherical object I carefully passed over the last time I was cleaning out the gutter on the roof? Perhaps it wasn't, as I thought at the time, left by a misguided swift. All kinds of creatures have been known to hatch from eggs – snakes, crocodiles, and the beast from twenty thousand fathoms. Perhaps it was dropped by a clumsy eagle as he flew over my house and even as I write crawly things are burrowing into the loft.

Elevators

The more you worry about elevators, the less often you travel in them and, unless you are already worrying about your heart condition and/or have cause to do so, walking upstairs is alleged to be good exercise. However, there are occasions, usually about the twelfth floor, when to summon the elevator may be thought desirable. Supposing that eventually it answers your summons and it is un-attended, your first worry is that the doors may imprison you within their grasp while you are still on the threshold. This is even more likely to occur if you are foolish enough to allow others to enter before you. On such occasions manners can make for quite a painful blow in the region of the kidney. Although the mechanism is supposed to be geared to your needs, it invariably wishes to demonstrate that it has a will of its own. Thus, after you have indicated a desire to be transported aloft, the elevator will decide to offer you the facilities of the floors below ground level before returning you, in the fullness of time, to your previous point of departure, after which, if it is by this point not overloaded, it may start upwards.

The elevator has now possibly imprisoned a fairly large collection of potential victims, each one alive to the danger that it may stop abruptly between floors and remain suspended for hours, days, and possibly even longer if the lift repairmen are not available owing to understaffing, more pressing repairs, or simply a strike. No one believes the emergency phone is manned. Survival plans are forming in the minds of most. The first worry is undoubtedly common to all – the call of nature and how to cope. The second is that there is very little room to stretch out, the third that these are not the sort of

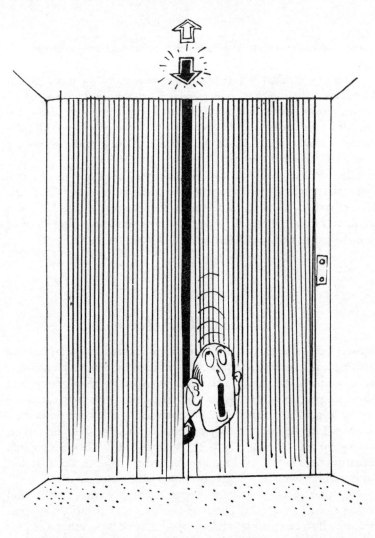

people one would normally choose to be stuck in an elevator with. While reminding yourself how much better this selection is usually done on the television, you may, if you are fortunate, have reached the floor you wished to visit. Remember to step out smartly – the same hazards confronting you when you started your journey still apply.

With lifts manned by attendants and operated by a rope, there is added a conviction that sooner or later you will find yourself dead at the bottom of the shaft, and you will worry if jumping wildly into the air at the moment of final contact with the basement will help. Manually operated elevators also develop, along with yourself, a sustained sideways tremor.

Sometimes you will find 'fun' lifts situated on the outside of buildings and travelling rapidly to revolving restaurants on top of towers. These have for the anxious all the excitement of a game of Russian roulette. Either you play Russian roulette or you don't. There is often a good bar at the base, together with a postcard kiosk.

Escalators

I always read the early warning notice displayed at the top of the moving staircase with every intention of obeying. I step on carefully, hold on to the rail, keep to the right while others skip by me, and take extravagant care to see that no article of my clothing can catch in the apparatus. I also try and separate myself from other passengers. I do not want a lady member of the House of Commons falling on top of me, as was the case recently. Luckily, on that occasion she made a soft landing on another member, but that sort of horseplay is better within government than outside it.

No, after the first hesitant step and the sensation of the land rising under one, I worry about an abrupt power failure or, supposing myself to be wearing sandals, which I am not, whether it is possible for the sole to be caught in the final tread and whether I could face life with an artificial foot. I should, of course, be worrying about what I did with the ticket but there will be time for that when I am once more on terra firma.

Exercise

Like sex some can never get enough of this. You only have to poke a head out of doors nowadays, even in extreme wintry conditions, to realize that many are engaged in a chilling marathon and that the rat race is increasingly competed for in the track suit. Those of us not as yet infected with the madness of the Gadarene swine can survey with a certain smugness the positioning of ambulances specializing in instant resuscitation at strategic points on city streets.

Once acquired, the habit of daily exercise becomes an obsession and men and women, deprived of their opportunity for running, skipping and jumping, visit to the sauna or squash court, or solitary tramp across the meadows, worry as they lie in hospital beds with broken limbs or suspected cardiac arrests until they can once more be up and about to strain yet another ligament or expire thankfully on the fifteenth green.

A man or woman who worries that he is not getting enough exercise leads a dog's life. The spectacle of a human being running after a ball and wagging his tail fills me with distaste. Exercise for the sake of exercise or in the hopeless quest of preservation is not to be countenanced in my book. The reader is advised to leave nature and not his friendly neighbourhood gymnasium instructor to count him out when the time comes. Cats once they cease to be kittens never take an unnecessary step and live longer than dogs, who do. You too will be better advised to stretch out in front of the fire and turn the page.

Families

To have one is to worry. Not to love your own mother will occasion as much anxiety as to love her too well. It takes enormous courage to dislike members of your own family to the point where you don't worry about them any more. It can be done but, alas, a man who has had his arm amputated still worries about the pain he feels in his elbow.

Feet

Some worry not only because their feet are not the right size but because they are not even the same size as each other. A lifetime of worrying about how to explain this to shoe-shop assistants is involved. Of all parts of the body feet are the most independent. Incorrigible trouble makers and hypochondriacal in the extreme, they register mysterious aches and pains which often don't add up to very much and then again may point to gout, athlete's foot or circulatory trouble developing literally overnight. A man is seldom at ease with his feet and often fears they will eventually encompass his downfall – hence the phrase, 'My feet are killing me.'

Getting them wet is a worry implanted in childhood which persists throughout life. To step inadvertently into a puddle or tall grass is to invite pneumonia. It is not, of course, simply a question of avoiding damp – feet are not, after all, made of sugar, and they have to be habitually bathed if you do not wish to worry that they may become offensive to others.

Putting one's foot in it is another constant anxiety to the careless conversationalist or pedestrian. One does not wish to end up with egg on one's face or something even more unpleasant on the sole of one's shoe.

Food

What to eat next rather than whom – since the practice of cannibalism was abandoned – is an abiding worry, shared alike by the hesitant shopper in the supermarket and the shipwrecked mariner rowing hopefully for the shore. The plight of the society hostess, consulting her book of recipes and trying to remember which of them comprised the menu on the last occasion when she entertained Russell Harty, is in sharp contrast to the exhausted seafarer choosing between the last can of bully beef or the last ship's biscuit, and again to the impoverished old-age pensioner foraging among this week's bargain offers of frozen Chinese pet foods.

Once a selection has been made, the preparation, cooking and serving of the stuff is an ensuing anxiety, along with the speed with which it is consumed if rations are meagre, or, in the hostess's case, how much is left on the plates. The planning of meals is a ceaseless worry, at least for those who can afford to serve them. The housewife is usually faced with one member of a family who dislikes curry. The dilemma is often simplified but never completely resolved by the purchase of yet another cookery book or the renewal of a prescription for Valium. The invention of instant foods and the removal from the dining-room table in preference for individual trays in front of the television screen is a partial solution and has done something to disperse parental worry about the table manners of their offspring. It also takes everyone's mind off what they are eating and transfers anxiety to the plight of Starsky and Hutch and deciding whether there is time to make a dash for the oven before the final shoot-out. A fairer atmosphere is also created. Father no longer gets the lion's share; he is also deprived of the privilege of worrying his children and his wife with his personal prejudices as to their conduct or the state of the economy while he carves the joint. What was once the traditional battleground, from which so many were expelled in disgrace or left never to darken the family door again, is now bare even of table-mats. Nevertheless, worry about food must occupy the minds of most people long after the traditional grace of childhood has failed to make them even remotely grateful for what they are about to receive.

As a baby is weaned from his mother's breast, he is confronted with a limited choice of prepared mushes and although at this age he is possibly unconscious of the wider choice he will hopefully encounter throughout adulthood, he will experience his first disappointment with banana-flavoured Cornish pasties and begin to worry lest another spoonful be crammed into his toothless and protesting gums, an experience likely to be repeated until he has learnt to spit meaningfully or when he finds himself approaching finality in the geriatric ward.

Next to deciding what to choose to eat, you will occasionally experience qualms and often certainty that what you have just eaten is likely to poison you. The agony of indecision is replaced on these occasions with the agony of indigestion and sometimes death. Oysters and mushrooms can be very worrying indeed, along with food still frozen towards the centre. Men seldom die these days from a surfeit of lampreys but it is surprising how many of us choke to death on steak. Some worry lest they find on their tongue a sliver of glass – glass, however, has to be powdered in order to be lethal – and others that food passed in the fingers means their host may be intent on poisoning them. Some even go so far as never to eat chocolates sent anonymously by post, at least until they have examined them for the pinprick of the hypodermic.

Foreign Travel

Potential worries here are so numerous that only a few can be touched on.

Language. A major anxiety is the inability of inhabitants of foreign countries to understand their native tongue.

Taxi drivers. These are simply not to be trusted, usually because of a pronounced death-wish, a deeply dishonest approach to what remains of life here on earth, a refusal to activate the meter, and a latent intention to find a quiet spot in the suburbs to ditch your corpse, having removed clothes and valuables.

Public transport. Not even the driver knows where the bus is bound for, but while you are worrying through which door to enter, he will have driven off. If you manage to get to the depot and find one unattended, you can climb aboard, though it is unlikely to be leaving for several hours. When it does so you will be unable to share your fellow passengers' refusal to realize that there are far too many aboard already and that frequent stops along the route to take on others will, supposing you survive suffocation, make it impossible for you to reach the exit when you imagine yourself to be in sight of the cathedral. The sooner you commence the struggle to emerge, the sooner you will find yourself once more alive but no longer kicking and in a part of the city you had previously no intention of exploring.

Finding your way on foot. Maps are largely useless, particularly when, as is usually the case, there is a military government in power. What to the map-maker was known at the time of going to press as the Boulevard Franklin Roosevelt is now the Avenue May 26th. There is also the worry of managing to refold it.

What to do. This is an excellent worry, especially if one realizes there is very little one can do or, indeed, wishes to do. Is there something wrong with me because I cannot take an interest in mediaeval Byzantine frescos partially restored. On the whole, better to find a convenient swimming pool, worry about the sun and the fact that you will probably never see the real Budapest, and how to give the impression you enjoyed yourself there when you return.

Shopping. How do they manage to pay those prices? No wonder everyone looks so shabby. Do they sell nothing in this country that isn't imported from Bath? Do I know anyone who still uses a toasting fork with a dragon for a handle? Why did I buy six postcards when I can't think of anything to write on any of them? Am I really having a good time? Why do I always find myself in places where tomorrow and the day after are public holidays?

See also Aeroplanes, Holidays, Sharks, Ships.

Forgetfulness

This is an all-purpose worry to be summoned at will, often at moments of contentment. For instance, it can add a spice of danger or excitement to the start of a journey. Have you remembered to close the bathroom window? Have you shut the cat in the greenhouse? You forgot to leave the back-door key in the accustomed hiding-place and Mrs Hoskins will be unable to let in the chimney sweep. 'Of course it matters,' you tell them, 'we must go back.' The cat is sitting on the dustbin, all the windows are shut and even as you enter the drive you remember Mrs Hoskins collected the back-door key herself. Now the worry is going to be whether you will catch the plane, for most of the journey you are wondering if you really packed your passport in the holdall and if so, whether the latter is really in the boot. You certainly didn't notice it sitting in the drive but then someone might have removed it. To give yourself something to do while waiting for a decision about the passport, you begin to count the children. 'I am,' you remark, 'afraid I am getting very forgetful.' Nobody will contradict you, though clearly nothing of the kind is the case. If you were, you wouldn't have remembered the cat.

Nature abhors a vacuum. Let us suppose you are looking forward to your holiday, which is why you have been worrying frantically for the last month that unforeseen circumstances, such as the bankruptcy of the travel agent, chicken pox or war with Andorra, may separately or even combined render it impossible at the last moment for you to take off. Those worries are now outgrown or may be once you are airborne, where a whole new set of worries will take over (*see* Aeroplanes). Meanwhile your worry needs will be met with a picnic hamper of anxiety to be partaken of lightly while the wheels are still turning. Will the fog clear? Is the roof-rack secure? Does it matter that the spare tyre is flat? If we pass the next ten cars without my seeing a bearded man in a mackintosh, this will be just about the best holiday we've ever had (*see* Omens). Once the airport is reached, you will find the passport is not in the holdall, which is hardly surprising since it is still where you put it – in your handbag.

The 'Did I Remember to Post the Letter?' syndrome is a self-imposed euphoria which can readily be brought into play when there is not a great deal going on and hence is a more or less continuing source of pleasurable distraction for the aged intent on reliving their few remaining hours. Time is passed not only putting the cat out but looking for pussy in the house after you have done so. Moreover, you will increasingly develop the worry of where you put down your glasses or the statement from the bank you were holding in your hand a moment ago. These time-consuming worries are, as we have observed, of immense benefit where there is time to consume and even if you are pressed for it, as many people often believe they are. How pleasurable to come across your spectacles where you left them, on the wash basin. How satisfying to find your gin and tonic only half consumed on the floor next to the television, and wasn't all that searching in the dustbin well worthwhile when you recovered the refund from the water rates? To be absent-minded at least postulates the possession of a mind and after it has temporarily withdrawn to reflect on some engrossing subject, you will be able to worry a good deal when trying to remember what the hell you were supposed to be thinking about.

Gambling

On this subject, happily, I am something of an expert. I have very much enjoyed all the resultant worries and sometimes I've managed to share them with family and friends. A peak worry period is always at six in the morning after an evening at a casino. Supposing you are already in bed, you will awake with a pleasurable feeling of remorse. You have, you tell yourself, been robbed but you yourself are the miscreant. No one else hit you over the head and made off with your ill-gotten gains.

As I am usually staying overnight in a hotel, my own recourse is to wake the staff, order a huge breakfast and search the papers for others in a worse plight than I. I could be a refugee stranded on the China Seas. Demonstrably they have lost more than I, and after the toast and marmalade I begin to worry about others. Any residual anxiety I still experience on my own account can be shared around ten o'clock with my bank manager. In the meantime I can write to the secretaries of all casinos resigning my membership and instructing them to refuse me admission in future. Luckily, I am not someone who carries a book of stamps around.

Games and Sports

This is the worry of not being picked for the side and, in my own case, that I might be. A child who displays the requisite aggression on the playing fields demanded by coach, schoolmaster and even, in some cases, parents will worry that he is not going to have a good match and will lose the captaincy forthwith.

The invention of the ball increased the worry potential of man almost as much as his discovery of a use for the wheel. A ball is thrown on the other side of the world and a man watching his television screen in Britain worries where it will land. You may worry that there is something very wrong with me that I cannot share his anxiety. Why am I unwilling to forgo my sleep to travel enormous distances overnight in pre-vandalized railway coaches to watch a team of my choice kick a football around in some alien stadium? Why do I not arm myself with flick-knife or broken bottle and, separated from the gladiators only by a wire fence, manfully try and climb over to gain a footing in the arena and stop the unequal contest? Is it simply because I am not there in the first place that I am powerless to express my fury over the conduct of the referee and linesmen and my continuing support for the side by smashing windows and brandishing my weapons all the way back to what may prove to be the police and not the railway station?

Why have I never tried to grasp a racket correctly or learned to swing a golf club, sought to pocket a billiard ball or survive a chukka, throw a dart or shove a halfpenny? It is because of a fear that once I started doing things like throwing a javelin around, there would be no stopping me. Surely I must become the best javelin hurler the world has ever known and would worry myself into an early grave fearful lest someone might snatch my crown. And which of all the games and sports in the world that I would automatically become champion of should I select? If I knew the answer, I could live longer by avoiding playing it. My worry is that I am not as yet certain. Until I am, I must avoid involvement with any.

Gardens

Wonderfully productive of worry at all stages of the life cycle, from early worries about mustard and cress refusing to grow on blotting paper to late ones as to whether you can afford to pay someone else to do the digging and cut the grass, and even if you can, is there

such a person available? Then there is the effect of early or late frost ruining your chance of a prize at the flower show, and the havoc wrought by nature's mercenaries – the mon rous regiment of snails, slugs, caterpillars, birds, rabbits, greenfly, moles, deer, squirrels and other unidentified creeping, crawling and flying objects – not to mention drought, flood, pestilence, and on occasions, if you have left a gate open, the very horsemen themselves engaged in hunting yet another of your natural foes, the fox.

Gardening is a high risk occupation and you may not worry until too late, when the fork has impaled your foot, the scythe cut you to the bone, the grass-cutter electrocuted you, the bonfire burnt down the house, the roller done lasting injury to your back, the greenhouse glass severed a tendon or a dead tree fallen gently on top of you. You will in all probability be too concerned over the unexpected death of a once thriving clump of lilies or the sickness of the vine which only last summer provided the grape jelly of which you were so proud, to avoid the peril.

You may be nearer to God in your garden than you ever imagined.

Gerbils

These little desert rats who pop about so cleverly are really very amusing. They are clean, non-smelly and fairly quiet, and would make an admirable pet for a worrier. They live in a cage so you always know where they are and they don't seem to overeat or have many nasty habits. They do, however, prefer to live in pairs and they do have very sharp incisors – used not as often for biting the hand that feeds them as for gnawing through almost anything. And that little book about small pets which every conscientious owner reads warns that if one pair of breeding gerbils should escape from domesticity, they would set up home in the wild and breed so prolifically that the havoc they would wreak on the harvest would make the biblical Egyptian seven-years famine seem but a moment. That bit of information can cause sleepless nights for any experienced worrier. Who, after all, would want to be responsible for the starvation of the world? There is a solution. Every home with a pair of gerbils should also have a cat. Then, if the cage should prove inadequate, nature will take its course. That, however, does not solve the dedicated worrier's problem. How many households have a pair of gerbils and no cat? Can agriculture hope to survive?

Habits

Thumb-sucking, leaving the door open, perpetually clearing the throat, omitting to remember when it's your turn to pay for a round of drinks, an inability to listen to what others are saying, failure to leave a newspaper or a tube of toothpaste in pristine condition, are more worrying when observed in other people than when practised by yourself.

The sight of a nun's habit recalls a pleasurable anxiety experienced during the last war when closer examination might prove the wearer to be an enemy agent recently parachuted behind our lines. The worry was how to achieve a closer examination and, if one's suspicions proved correct, what to do about it. I find this worry still persists, but since most nuns are now dressed by Marks and Spencers it is not, alas, as common as far as I am concerned. There are, of course, fewer enemy parachutists around but, luckily, more transvestites.

Holidays

Planning for these is often a pleasurable worry. It is only when the decision has been arrived at that morbid worry commences. Contrary to all expectation, the journey is accomplished without mishap and, with only a light drizzle falling, things could be worse. True, the sea is not quite where you expected it to be and the beach accessible only by an underpass, but the swimming pool looks comparatively clean. While you search the luggage for the portable iron you have somehow omitted to pack, you try to figure out the angle from which the photograph on the brochure advertising the hotel could possibly have been taken. Later that evening, when your brood has not been kidnapped as you feared but discovered in the shopping arcade, you will share your husband's dismay at the price of the local wine and imported spirits, order Eau Minérale, and listen as calmly as possible to the barman's assurance that with the wind in the direction it has assumed there is little chance of fine weather until the new moon. At least the children won't get sunstroke and the shrine of the Black Madonna is only thirty kilometres away.

Luckily there are other worries available. The children don't seem to have made any suitable friends other than the waiter. No one seems to understand that your youngest will scream at mealtimes unless something is produced for her to chew on after ten minutes at the table. Immature squid is difficult to appreciate, the absence of green vegetables may lead to an outbreak of scurvy and neither the bedroom curtains or the television are as adequate as they are back home. With luck you will soon be back there.

Horses

An animal almost incapable of looking after itself is a constant source of worry to those who possess, bet on, try to breed from, and finally to dispose of at a profit. It is possible to teach a child, particularly if she is a girl, horse worry at an early age by encouraging her to accompany the creatures in horse-boxes to local meets and gymkhanas. On their return, the horse will have to be bedded down for the night in its stall and the child in the local cottage hospital.

For those of my readers who have nothing particularly to worry about and cannot conveniently spend their incomes, I recommend a large family racing or hunting stable, with the possibility of accommodating from time to time one or more stallions and some brood mares. In the children's early and formative years, there will also have to be ponies. It would need a completely separate volume to list the potential number of worries you will then be able to experience at first hand or even vicariously, lying on an orthopaedic bed, or while propelling yourself from race-track to race-track in your invalid chair, pen gripped firmly in your teeth as you sign the cheques in payment of hospital and veterinary bills.

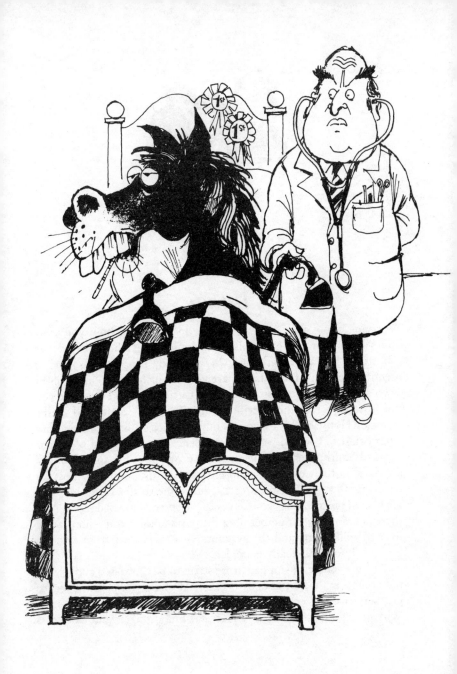

Image

Worrying about your image – and I do not mean how you view yourself in a mirror, though this too is conducive of a host of anxieties – but who you are exactly and why so many people are unable to identify you. Why, for instance, are you not included in the pages of *Who's Who* or on the lists of the royal Garden Parties? Why are you not invited to face the television cameras or be entertained in the Mansion House? Why are you merely included among those without whom statistics would be a barren science? In the world of Logan Pearsall Smith, there are just so many of you who annually take holidays on the Costa Brava, lose just so many umbrellas, post an exact number of Christmas cards, subscribe to the *National Geographic Magazine*, offer yourselves as blood and kidney donors. And there is even a fixed number of enthusiasts among you who get run over by milk-floats and throw yourselves every year from London bridges. But is this really enough?

Why are you never stopped in the street to be canvassed about your preferences in the matter of detergents? Why are you passed over for jury service or never appointed to a committee of typical road users? Why are you not accosted by Hari Krishna disciples and can cross picket lines without being offered a leaflet concerning the claims of the strikers?

Take heart, gentle reader. This worry is dedicated to you and you alone.

Insurance

Although insurance companies allow little margin for worry about the compensation to be paid for losing one's life in an accident on a railway line or on the ocean bed, and also offer advantageous (albeit fixed) rates for sustaining, say, the loss of one arm and one limb below the knee or alternatively two eyes and one limb above the elbow, the loss assessed when your house is burnt down or you electrocute yourself at play is left to be fixed by an individual. A profitable worry hour can thus be spent evaluating the exact sum to be claimed towards the cost of rebuilding and refurbishing the property after the holocaust, always provided that it is not a natural holocaust. Flooding, earthquakes and cosmic rays are specifically excluded from most insurances. The companies dislike them almost as much as war and civil uprisings. Worries about these are thus better indulged separately.

As inflation mounts, insurance cover must be increased along with the premium demanded. Even while reading this last sentence the better class reader will experience a frisson of unease, reminding himself that tomorrow he must once again tackle the problem of ascertaining the exact worth of the infinitely doubtful Sickert he brought back in triumph from Tunbridge Wells. Even if no very definite provenance is yet established, the cornerstone of his collection hasn't even been listed separately. The real worry of insurance is obviously whether you win in the end. Over-insure and you will have to sell the stuff anyway to pay the premium. Under-insure and you will no longer be living in quite the style you had imagined when you struck the match. Defrauding an insurance company is a serious matter. There is simply no way an insurance company can defraud you. All that happened was you didn't read the small print.

Life insurance too is a gamble in which the odds are loaded against you. All I want, I will tell myself during the hours I ponder these matters, is that when I go, they will be well looked after. They, in this context, can mean a wife and family for whom up to now I have provided, and/or in some cases (but not my own) a couple of mistresses in Maida Vale, a faithful outdoor and indoor staff and a small herd of donkeys for whom one has purchased a meadow. Even if things do not work out quite as we had planned, we will at least have left them something to worry about, along with whatever cash is available after death duties (*see* Death Duties).

Irrational Impulses

Here are three worries in one – or so swiftly following upon each other's heels that they appear to be. First, a sudden, overwhelming desire to count up to ten very loud indeed is fulfilled in Chichester Cathedral. Have you been overheard and if so, will fellow worshippers or sightseers imagine you were testing for echoes? Worry number two is that, having given in to one irrational impulse, can you continue to resist the desire you have at times to push a complete stranger to his death on the live rail of the tube? Worry three, what sort of person are you who entertains such bizarre fancies? Atavism, you tell yourself, is what accounts for it. Primordial passion perhaps caused some remote ancestor to plunge the knife into one of his guests instead of carving the meat and you have inherited the craving. Sunday has been a happy day up to now, but how long can it last?

What would happen if while driving along the narrow and elevated roadway connecting the Staines bypass to the A4, I direct the motor, as I have so often considered doing, into those flimsy-looking barriers and land triumphantly on the road beneath? Most actors have an impulse to suddenly hurl four-letter expletives at their captive audience. Since this impulse normally arises at a certain point in the action of the play, each time they approach flash-point thereafter the temptation grows a little stronger. It may not happen the night you are in the audience, it may never happen, but if you are suddenly conscious that concentration seemed momentarily to falter, it might be worth going back a bit later in the run. You could be present at a happening.

I have, of course, experienced the temptation myself, but on the other hand my approach to picture galleries is more mature. I seldom have the urge to slash a masterpiece and never the weapon required to do so, which doesn't protect me from the desire on occasions to hurl a sculpture to the ground or punish a pile of plates tastefully stacked in a store. Once, returning from a trip from Paris I chanced to sit next to a celebrated dealer in Russian snuff boxes and remembered having read of the vast sums he had paid in an auction the day before for one of Mr Fabergé's *folies de grandeur*. 'You don't happen to have it on you?' I enquired, and he tossed the treasure wrapped up in newspaper into my lap. 'This is it,' I told myself. Only the fact that we were travelling by air and not by rail prevented the supreme gesture of a lifetime. I did once hold an even more precious object in my clammy palm, Miss Taylor's diamond no less, but the urge to run with it off the studio floor and disappear into the Moscow underground can scarcely be considered irrational. All I worried bout was that the opportunity would never occur again in more favourable circumstances – and it never has up to now.

Jam

One morning, instead of worrying why the papers haven't arrived yet again, try reading the label on the jam jar. You read the list of ingredients. Sugar – fine. Strawberries – lovely. Glucose syrup – isn't that some kind of sugar? But there's already sugar in it. Pectin – that's all right, it's the gooey stuff that makes it all congeal. Fruit acid – what's that? Why isn't it in strawberries and, if it isn't, why does it have to be in strawberry jam? Sodium citrate. Sodium citrate? That sounds very nasty, but the worst is yet to come. Preservative, it says. But it doesn't say what the preservative is. If they boldly list something as horrid-sounding as sodium citrate, why are they ashamed to tell us what the preservative is? And finally you come to colour. Wasn't there a long article in the newspaper the other week about red colouring causing cancer in rats? Try reading labels on other foods when you are at a loss for what to worry about next.

Alternatively, try home-made jam. This is the result of the worry over what to do with the glut of strawberries you've grown or the blackberries the children have collected. It is a satisfying activity in itself, producing worry over whether it will set properly, where you will get enough jars to contain it (have you sterilized them properly?) and finally, what is that green fuzz which has grown on top of it after six weeks in the cupboard? Has it also appeared on the three dozen jars you sold at the church fête and the other two dozen you so happily disposed of as presents far and wide?

Kidnapping

In early childhood I was aware of the danger of being kidnapped by gipsies. It was a theme much favoured by novelists and makers of silent films. Over the years I had begun to smile tolerantly at the predicament of my own mother-in-law, Gladys Cooper, in her portrayal on celluloid of *The Bohemian Girl*. How well she coped with being reared Romany fashion, how remote the possibility that gipsies these days could even afford one extra mouth to feed. Alas, the gipsies have returned and kidnapping is an ever-present worry to those engaged in the diplomatic service and in trade with emerging nations. It is no longer any use pretending that it is not an anxiety shared by the very rich and all those entrusted overnight with the keys of the office safe.

In the extremely unlikely event that anyone should want to kidnap me I am convinced that I should remain brave and calm. I should by my very fortitude and the manifest inability, indeed possible reluctance, of my family to find the ransom, eventually win the hearts of my captors and my own freedom in return. It is only the possibility of being carried from my bed down an extremely awkward staircase by a required minimum of four assailants that fills me with temporary and utter panic.

Knocks on the Door

These provide endless opportunities for worry. It could be anyone from an armed bank robber in search of a hostage to the gentleman from the pools. More probably it is a confused motorist demanding directions.

The single knock suggests that you have more to gain from answering the summons than the knocker himself. The more peremptory the tapping, the less chance that there is anything in it for yourself. It could be the police with a search warrant or, on the other hand, they might merely wish to advise you of flames issuing from an upstairs window or of a decision by the Gas Board to evacuate the area because of a suspected break in the mains.

A more prolonged and cheerful rat-a-tat-tat indicates the possible proximity of friends or relatives anxious to stay the night. You may sit this one out but unless you have taken the precaution of having a peephole installed in your front door, you will worry for the rest of the day whether it wouldn't have been kinder to have gone to the trouble of making up the spare bed and availing yourself of a spare ticket to the flower show or Frank Sinatra.

A knock on the back door, however, is almost reassuring. It usually means that something you are expecting has, contrary to your expectations, actually arrived. There will be little necessity to entertain the bearer. Neighbours in search of milk can be dealt with summarily. If woken from sleep by persistent hammering, do not pull the bedclothes over your head before first ascertaining that you have not inadvertently locked out a member of your own family.

Lavatory Seats

Originally conceived as a daring alibi for the less pleasant results of sexual promiscuity, the idea of catching something nasty in the wood-shed or from public toilets persists. However carefully you may select your cubicle, however scrupulously you wipe and polish, you will not rest easy on the throne. However, once the plug is pulled and the lavatory vacated, the worry tends to recede until next time. Some people actually go through life without incurring infection but none without worry about the risk of doing so.

Life after Death

There is still a considerable body of opinion convinced that paradise exists and, once gained, holds no further worries of any kind. Such a privilege has to be earned by consistently indicating intense gratitude to the provider of the celestial haven and communicating unstinted admiration for the arrangements being made for reception into the

life hereafter. Although God, unlike Father Christmas, is seldom actually written to, telegraphed, or rung up, he is held to listen attentively to supplication or praise delivered silently or in many languages, the voices often being accompanied by ritual chanting or music of one kind or another. Almost all religions agree that God is fond of music, sometimes of dancing, and always of processions.

The conception of heaven often brings with it one of purgatory and, although it is no longer as fashionable as it was to conceive of eternal retribution being exacted from the damned, many religions still instruct their members to be a shade careful when mixing with, or emulating the customs of, non-members. They can thus worry extensively about the perils of mixed marriages, proscribed diets, ceremonial circumcision, the education of their children and which particular days of the month or year should be set aside for worship and abstinence from carnal and domestic tasks. They can also worry, but not perhaps as much as they might, about the eventual fate of others who have either not seen the light or, what is considered even worse, strolled deliberately off into the surrounding darkness.

A deeply-felt religious conviction, whether experienced by the Holy Father himself, a Mormon missionary, or a lecturer on the fundamental beliefs of a British Israelite, though it brings consolation to some, occasions at times prodigious worry in the minds of the unconverted. A study of comparative religions can be highly recommended to such readers. This most beneficial and time-consuming puzzle increases the worry potential and up to the time of going to press provides no final solution as to which religion the Almighty himself prefers.

See also Burial, alive

Locks

These are instant reminders to worry about having forgotten, or worse still, lost the key of the front door, the car, the desk, the drawer, the cash box or safe, the prison cell – and if you haven't exactly lost them, where did you put them down? Then in your pocket there is the key of the hotel you have already left. Will it really go into any pillar-box without doing damage to mail already deposited? (Not your worry.)

If you are on a river, you will encounter locks all too soon. Long before the gates approach you will be assessing the danger and dreading the scorn of the lock-keeper and other boatmen. It is little use telling your passengers to hold on to the chains. Sooner or later lack of concentration or ability will cause your craft to swing round and attack the other punts or launches. If you are a river lock worrier, better to turn the boat round before entering. The water looks exactly the same on the other side.

Loneliness

A common, almost vulgar worry readily available to all throughout their life span, it is nowadays a growth industry. Whereas in the past loneliness was held to be the prerogative of kings and clowns, now it is associated with long-distance runners and everyone who advertises in the personal columns of the daily, weekly or monthly press. Thoreau's reflection that he had never found a companion that was so companionable as solitude, or Swift's that a wise man is never less alone than when he is alone, simply cut no ice today. Next to worrying that you are lonely yourself and can count your true friends on less than one hand, there is the worry of others' loneliness, people who may in their turn be worrying about yours. The roads of Britain are full of charabancs conveying elderly sufferers of the lonely hearts syndrome to Bognor Regis to take their minds off their lonely plight and give them fresh worries as to whether the sun will be shining or about the singular lack of public lavatories when they arrive.

Love

Falling in love is the result of being pushed by ourselves or others. Love is a self-inflicted worry which, like the bed in which it is consummated, is sometimes king-size. Falling out may cause a nasty bump.

There is a temptation to spread love worries into the appropriately named agony columns of the media when difficulties arise. Sob sisters usually dry the tears but not always. A man who recently fell in love with his own father-in-law and wrote to say he had every reason to suppose his feelings were reciprocated, got short shift from Abby in the *Miami Herald*. 'Try not to meet too frequently,' she chided.

Some fall in and out of love a hundred times; for others the worry is not to be born more than once. Either these people settle for what they hope will be peaceful co-existence or draw the blind, bolt the door and never venture out down lover's lane again. There is neither need, nor space, to list the worries available for lovers. The most inexperienced, however carefree, will find their quiver full of worry arrows ready to be fired from Cupid's bow.

Loved Ones

This could be the night your house burns down or your family is attacked by marauders as you are drinking the loyal toast some distance away. Every mile on the homeward journey increases the presentiment of horrendous disaster. At the very least a child is now in hospital with a grumbling appendix, your wife by his bedside, with the other children, wrapped in blankets and bleary-eyed apprehension, keeping vigil in the night sister's office.

You picture your family grouped around the television when it suddenly bursts into flames which engulf the house, or answering a knock at the door to find themselves the hostages of a gunman on the run. A pack of mad dogs is even now hurling itself against the French windows, a flight of ravenous starlings is alighting one after another on the hearth, and poisonous spiders are mustering for battle in the bath. None of this could possibly be happening, you tell yourself as you turn the last corner of the road, or I would have been stopped a mile back by a police car – unless, of course, they haven't yet discovered what's been going on. There are no fire engines in the drive, no ambulances, not even a Panda car, but only half reassured, you open the door to find the house in darkness and all your loved ones asleep. Brandy is a powerful aid to this anxiety – so for that matter is indigestion.

Marriage

A cliff-hanger of a worry, at least until the wedding breakfast and more often than not for many years afterwards. Marriage is a status symbol for many women, to achieve which they are prepared to take appalling risks and often to subject themselves to a lifetime of disappointment. A man's decision to marry is the acceptance of a calculated risk, arrived at after experiencing a comparable amount of worry to that which his intended has undergone. He has reached the age when he definitely wishes to extend his worry potential and involve himself with life beyond his means and a wife and eventually children beyond his control.

Once a decision as to the wedding date has been made, there is for all within range a vast explosion in the worry field, scattering anxiety debris in every direction and involving those in the immediate vicinity and even those on the distant perimeter in the ensuing holocaust – florists, caterers, clergy, printers, dressmakers, best and second-best friends, bell-ringers, bank managers, travel agents, etc., etc., etc. Even so, there will be long periods of the working day or sleepless night when both partners will be able to agonize without interruption over whether it would not be wiser to call the whole thing off. Cancellation is usually too awesome to think about, involving, as it well might, returning the wedding gifts, an action for breach of promise, being sent to Coventry by those who might think you had behaved badly or being seen off to Melbourne by those who believe you have taken the wiser course.

The wedding ceremony is an operation mercifully performed under anaesthetic. Waking up in the marriage bed next morning there is first a sense of relief that it is over and then the anxiety that some vital organ has been removed. What happens next is anyone's guess, but a marriage in which the partners share the same worries is bound to result in them both eventually worrying about divorce proceedings. If one partner worries about money, punctuality, career, physical fitness, going bald, hi-fi equipment, insurance policies, school bills, sexual prowess, washing the car, bank loans and the price index, while the other worries about clothes, amateur theatricals, prevention of blood sports, neighbours, shopping facilities, meals on wheels, whooping cough and whether the goldfish is the only one who might be happier with sex in the afternoon and decides to buy another – there is always hope for all three.

Money

Unless you decide to blow your brains out, drive your car over a cliff, lie down on some convenient stretch of railway line or shop extensively at the local chemist, there is no way in which you can deprive yourself of the pastime of worrying about money. Philosophers believe it was invented to take man's mind off the impermanence of life. It is a preoccupation first encountered in childhood when you are initiated into this almost universal custom by the presentation of a money-box or the opening of a savings account by eager parents. You are thus taught almost from birth that you will never have enough of the stuff to buy what you need in life. You may be content for a short time to rattle your money-box or to be told that you have seventeen pounds in the post office but very soon the pen-knife will be inserted into the slit and the last stamp surrendered and the train set purchased. The money-box will never rattle again and you will be off on your bicycle to deliver the newspapers in order to afford a new one. You will have joined the eternal slate club of life.

For some the worry of money is so deeply ingrained in childhood that they continue to count it each evening, long after they have ceased to say their prayers and it no longer becomes necessary for them to brush their teeth. They will make a neat pile of the loose change and folded paper in their pockets and then record the sums spent during the day. Supposing them to be able to add and subtract correctly, they will be able to account for some but by no means all the expenditure they have incurred since getting out of bed. They can then worry about having been short changed at the supermarket or the inflationary spiral performed by a packet of cornflakes.

Most people do not need so strict a discipline to become and remain money worriers. Although they may never know their exact balance or overdraft (preferring to cash their cheques anywhere but at their bank, thus avoiding the puzzled cashier disappearing towards the manager's office and the subsequent invitation to step inside for coffee and biscuits), they will realize that they are now and always will be deeply insolvent and that worry is the penance they must undergo for the sin of extravagance. Most believers limit not only the frequency but the time spent in the confession box but in old age there is a temptation to use it as a permanent base. Over-indulgence is not recommended either at this or any other stage of life. To live with money worry is one thing. To be found in your own spinney with a discharged shot-gun beside you will invite the coroner to remark merely that the deceased appeared to have financial problems, almost as pointless an observation as noting that like most of us you used to have a head on your shoulders.

Names

'How lovely to see you after all this time. How's the family? Did she, I'm sorry, but the others? No, of course not, how silly of me. I was thinking for a moment you had a cousin in Calais. And you still live in the old place, where you used to I mean? Well, it obviously suits you, you don't look a day older. They were great days, I often think of them, great happy days, and we still have the memory of them, they can't take that away from us.... Do you ever go back to Frinton? Oh. Memory does play tricks on one, but I am right, surely, you did marry Delia? You didn't? Look, you are simply never going to believe this, but I haven't the foggiest idea who you are. You see, I had this rather bad fall a few years ago and it's left the most extraordinary gaps in my memory. The other day I actually failed to recognize my own brother-in-law. What's that? ... Let me get you a drink.

'Ah, Mrs Lorimer, this is a pleasant surprise. It was so nice of you to come. Did you bring your husband? Yes, I know he's dead, I just meant, do you still feel him around you? I don't know, it was just a crazy idea of mine. Good old Harry, he always loved a party. How extraordinary, he always seemed to be enjoying himself whenever I saw him at one. I know that's what he'd like you to do, go on enjoying life. You intend to now he's finally gone. Oh, well done!'

Nation, state of the

A continuing and open-ended worry capable of limitless expansion, it has the enormous advantage of being communicable to others and of all the worries in this book, this is the one I most confidently recommend, although it's not suitable for children. Examples:

Honesty is the last thing attributable to politicians and, come to that, to almost anyone who ventures to send in a bill or demands payment in cash. The vast majority of fellow citizens are demonstrably greedy and untrustworthy: either they don't deliver the goods or, if they do, they overcharge outrageously. Promises are made to be broken these days, and in affairs of the heart and the bed they are often not even voiced. The criminal underworld, like the extension of the Ealing Line, has emerged into broad daylight. Jack no longer even thinks himself as good as his master – he is his master. The chip on his shoulder is now made of silicon. A man masters the keyboard of the computer only to discover it has no further use for his services. Oil recovered from the bed of the ocean spills over to suffocate the seagulls and very soon the inhabitants of Bournemouth. The little pig changed his mind about going to the Common Market and hasn't been seen since. When you speak of the Welfare State what you are really describing is the Farewell State – no wonder the former Governor of the Bank of England now lives in Jersey. I wish I could join him.

If you reluctantly decide to stay in Britain you will never be at a loss for a topic of conversation.

Neighbours

Neighbours, whether they live beside you, on top of you, beneath you, or, if you are the fortunate possessor of a detached house, within a quarter of a mile of you, always provoke deep anxiety. The Englishman who has just found somewhere to live is immediately apprehensive lest life in his new abode should be rendered impossible by the presence of other people playing music far into the night, attacking each other with knives, not keeping children or pets under control, invading his privacy, not calling to wish him well, being stuck up or run down, parking cars, dustbins, prams, erecting garages or garden sheds, altering their greenhouses, giving parties, constructing swimming pools, not painting their front doors, or by doing so spoiling the look of the terrace, hanging washing, not taking in the milk. The best worry is not having any neighbours at all for a brief period while the sale of adjacent premises is being negotiated. However unsatisfactory the last occupiers, the next are almost sure to be worse.

Making friends with your neighbours leads to further anxiety on their account or your own. The closer you grow together, the greater the danger of them simply not bothering to buy a deep-freeze, or hire a competent baby-sitter. As if you hadn't enough worries of your own, you will now find yourself deeply, albeit sometimes pleasurably, immersed in the complications which are bound to ensue should you take the advice of loving your neighbour too literally. There are almost certain to be other neighbours who will spill the beans. Time, you may tell yourself, to make a clear break and to begin to worry how this can be achieved without arousing your own spouse's suspicions.

As for coveting your neighbour's worldly possessions, you may begin to be resentful not only of his life-style but his refusal to divulge how he manages to run three motor cars, maintain a villa in Capri and a mistress in Torremolinos, send his children to public schools and purchase the latest in video tape-recording. Better

perhaps to forget about him and concentrate on worries envisaged by the neighbour on the other side who is chairman of the local residents' association, ever eager to involve you in demonstrations in favour of additional pedestrian crossings, or against demolition orders on local windmills.

Other neighbours may give you cause for concern, such as the recluse about whom no one appears to know anything except that her front garden is a disgrace and she is reported to have a fortune secreted on the premises. Should you try and make friends with her cats? Stranger things have happened than codicils made at the last moment leaving a large fortune to anyone proven to have been fond of cats and willing to keep them in the style to which they are accustomed. Quite apart from these considerations, she might die unobserved and the coroner have harsh things to say about the selfishness of the uncaring some months later. Again, is there something very strange about the couple who only seem to go out at dusk? Are they merely working as part-time croupiers or is there substance in your suspicions that they are members of a sleeping IRA cell? Is a word to the local police station in order or might your telephone call not be treated as confidentially as promised?

Newspapers

Despite their ostensible faith in bums and tits, newspaper proprietors know full well that what sells a paper is worry, and more worry. On the days when newspapers suspend publication, there is a definite feeling of unidentifiable loss among their would-be readers. This is worry loss, and what the public is suffering from is worry withdrawal symptoms. Unless people are reminded every morning of the Whitby Jones forecast of a severely depressed toffee industry in the 1980s, the latest casualty figures caused by Basque Separatists, the imminent decline of amateur badminton, the state of motorway cafés, and the almost total extinction of poplars in Battersea Park, they tend to cease worrying about them. The public must be constantly able to read what has gone wrong, is wrong and will almost certainly be going wrong in the near future. The reader is prepared to share the editor's misgivings, doubts and anxiety, and make them his own. On the other hand, Miss Motor Bicycle 1980 looks, and indeed is, out of his grasp, although some may worry that among the things she is not wearing is a crash-helmet.

Omens

An ancient and obsessional worry which survives and flourishes. Now that the temples where the priests interpreted the portents are in ruins, modern man has resorted to fixing the signs for himself. The commuter on his daily walk to the station is convinced that if he reaches the next pillar-box before being passed by a cyclist, he will be apprised that very morning of his promotion. When he is pipped at the box by a head bent low over the handlebars, he refuses to abandon hope. 'I naturally ruled out racing cyclists,' he tells himself, 'the job's still on in my opinion.'

Oracles have been manipulated since time immemorable. Thus a man who has decided a fortune will be his tomorrow if he can make a four-letter word from the registration letters of any of the next seven cars he overtakes is not too disappointed if he fails to do so. Strictly against the rules he decides that the original number he hit on was not a fair test.

Only when the oracle consulted appears to be really aware of his duty does worry burgeon. If, when reaching the end of this pier, I once told myself, I should spy a one-armed lady without a hat feeding the seagulls, I shall be dead in the morning. It was just possible that she had the other arm in a sling concealed under her coat. Obviously such must have been the case as I am still alive to tell the tale.

Parties

Why wasn't I asked? This is a childhood worry which, if cherished, can last long past middle age. In your early eighties, however, you will find you are automatically invited by assorted friends of geriatrics and if you do manage to get to the party, you will be able to start to worry how you are going to get home. Party givers seldom realize that before the ink is dry on the invitation cards, they have started a chain of anxiety common to host and invited alike. To go or not to go?

In very early life the decision is usually made by the parent and, until a child is old enough to understand all the implications involved, he may even enjoy a few spoonfuls of jelly and a paper hat around a neighbour's dining-table. He will not be expected to talk or make friends. He can even be sick over his hostess. But in a few years things are different; a code of manners is beginning to be imposed. He will have to arrive tidily dressed, with a present which, although it didn't cost him anything, he would dearly have liked to retain and, indeed, is ready to snatch back once it has been unwrapped. He will not be allowed to get away with it. Life will teach him a sharp lesson – winner takes all. It may also teach him that he is liable to get thumped by strangers, lose out at musical chairs and not be chosen as the sorcerer's apprentice.

Worrying about going to parties at all is best indulged in by teenagers. Will they notice my spots? Will anyone want to dance with me? Why haven't I a dinner-jacket of my own, or even a girl? Will they realize I failed my 'O' levels? Can I safely pretend to have seen *Evita*? Once acquired, the habit of worrying about any function you have to attend is easy to cultivate. Tell yourself something could go wrong from the moment you accept. You might appear on the wrong day. A journey to the drawing-room mantelpiece to verify the date is

worthwhile even in the middle of the night – it could have been that very evening. What to wear? What time to arrive? Will you know anyone? Will you hear properly? Should you have a stiff drink beforehand? Why have they asked you? You are at the top table, and both your neighbours have turned away to talk to their neighbours. How long can you pretend to be judging the Beaujolais, finishing the quiche? You could be in the middle of dinner and suddenly develop gastro-enteritis. There is always a first time for everything.

Wife-swapping parties are often non-starters but if they do come off, they bring a veritable host of new worry problems. If there were four men and four women, how come I had to manage on my own? If Roger, as he claimed, had never been in the house before, how did he know where we kept the table tennis equipment? Who sent us the red light bulb? What was the police car doing parked at the end of the

road the next evening. Who sent Nora the flowers with the inscription, 'Thanks for the happy event, hope we won't have to wait too long for the next one?' Are we going to have a baby at last? That will be the end of that worry at least.

Pickpockets

An increasing problem that causes men to distribute the load over as many as a dozen or more pockets that they have about them, thus spreading the worry load every time they try and find a handkerchief or a Diners Card. In pulling out the handkerchief, care must now be exercised lest they pull out the traveller's cheque. Tailors have abandoned the hip-pocket with button flap – too vulnerable they tell us – thereby saving the work. Even the gentlest brush by a stranger in the High Street causes the confirmed male worrier to disappear up a side alley or into a cubicle of a public lavatory to check what is left.

For ladies who still persist in putting all their eggs in one handbag, the latter must be firmly clutched at all times and the clasp furnished with a padlock. Now all they have to really worry about is what they did with the key, or, in the event that they have invested in one furnished with a combination lock, whether they can remember the combination.

Pickpockets themselves worry lest their work should have been in vain.

Post

Letters described as 'in the post' are the easiest to worry about. In the first place they almost certainly aren't. The phrase is a minor euphemism, meaning that you are not going to get the money or the confirmation of employment. But maybe the letter has been lost, or misdirected. No, you checked the address when you phoned. Your solicitor has simply decamped with all your securities, the firm are not going to refund your money – ever, your putative employers have changed their minds, your friend has no intention this time of paying back the loan. Plenty of unpleasant alternatives as to your future course of action present themselves. Should you drive the car without an insurance certificate, and if caught, can you be sent to prison? With your credit card lost, there will be no food in the house by Wednesday. Could you have received your credit card, failed to open the envelope because you thought it was the account, and thrown it unopened into the boiler? It's all the fault of the computer. What the world is crying out for is an all-out attack on computers. Could you organize this? Why doesn't the postman care any more, or is he one of those who doesn't like walking, takes the mail home and hides it?

Letters you expected, not designated by anyone as being in the post but which simply haven't arrived, are almost as worrying. Why haven't you heard from Charles? When he first went to Durham he wrote every week. Could he have met with an accident? Joined the Foreign Legion? Decided to drop out and is sitting quietly smoking himself to death? Could he be working at last? Has he been sent down and got a job on the railways? What if he has been killed in the shunting yard? Let us leave Charles and consider the girl you met in the British Museum (you are younger now) and who promised to write. Why the hell didn't you get her address? Did she mean what she said about a fortnight in Yugoslavia together? Admittedly it was your suggestion, but did she agree to it just to get rid of you? Did she think you were just another sex maniac? Are you just another sex maniac? If so, what should you do about it? Why not forget her?

But you don't want to forget her, you just want to sit there and worry about her. The one woman who could have made you happy.

Why does no one write to you (you are any age now)? Other people get letters from friends. How many friends have you got? There must be more if only you could remember. How can you expect letters if you don't write any yourself? But won't they think it odd suddenly to hear from me? Should I buy a lot of picture postcards and send them to people I would like to write back? Of course, I'd have to go somewhere to post them. Zurich. 'Am here for a few days, it's a very pretty town.' Is Zurich a pretty town? How about Bournemouth? Nobody sends cards from Bournemouth. Still, it might puzzle them. 'Why is he in Bournemouth?' they'll wonder, 'let's write and find out.' Of course I'd have to let them know I was only there for a short stay, otherwise they'd think I'd moved. Where from? Do they have my permanent address? 'If you want to get in touch, this will find me.' Why should they want to get in touch? They never have before.

Perhaps the most serious worry of all, though, are the letters which really are in the post and will be on the breakfast table in the morning – gas board, inland revenue, recorded delivery from Luton Magistrates Court, Whychwood School, bank manager, rating authority. Legal and General, telephone company, electricity board. But surely they can't all come at once? They can, you know, they can and will. What is the house going to be like without heat, light and telephone, bailiffs to be fed and the children? Should you go downstairs and turn on what's left of the gas?

Restaurants

The search for the right one is now, thanks to their proliferation, a most pleasurable source of anxiety. I am no longer content with the little bistro round the corner. Like everyone else, I know there is now another round the next corner, and the next, and so on ad infinitum. Useless to remind myself that if the proprietor doesn't already know me as a customer, he may not even want to do so. The fact that all the tables are already taken or, even worse, vacant but reserved, spurs anxiety to gain a foothold even if it means a long and sometimes hopeless wait at the bar. Meanwhile, I am constantly consulting a library of guidebooks as to which others to choose and subsequently patronize. In one the bouillabaisse is apparently tasty but clients fail to agree on the quality of the syllabub. The difficulty for me here is I don't care much for fish soups but adore puddings. Some appear to be not as good as they were, others to be gaining at least in the size of the portions. Manifestly, this is not the right moment to essay any of these. There is so much that has to be taken into consideration. Where on earth is Mackerel Street and how do I recognize Mr Suliman when I arrive? Other customers, of course, have the advantage of remembering him when he was based in Lavinia

Gardens but I am not, alas, among them. Another offering plain, simple food on scrubbed trestle-tables must be ruled out because diners are subjected to an accordion player late in the evening.

All in all it is a most worrying choice, only marginally helped by the perusal of yet another authority who boldly lists at least a hundred establishments which have failed to meet its standards. Finally, you tell your guests you have a treat in store for them. You are trying an entirely new venue where the tables are set with white cloths, inoffensive Victorian lamps, a flower in a brandy glass and a napkin folded like a lily. When you arrive the restaurant is entirely empty, which creates a fresh worry as to whether you have made the right choice. However, you can take a bold line, announce you were expecting to meet Mr Zingwall and since, as it now appears, he hasn't made a reservation, you will just pop out again in search of him, but will return later.

There is always at least one of the party who worries so much about what to eat that he or she is unable to order anything for some time. Do not attempt to ease this worry. Only silence will eventually resolve it – if you are lucky before the kitchens close.

If you are in the unfortunate position of having to pay the bill, estimate the possible total and double it. Then double it again. The shock when it arrives will thus be lessened by approximately ten per cent.

There are so many worries associated with eating out, such as the choice of wine, who sits next to whom, whether your entire table is not too close to the kitchen, how to get the conversation going and later how to bring it to a close, and whether the waiter who helps you on with your coat is the same one who served the meal and if not, whether yet another tip is required, that you will get to bed well satisfied that you have exercised your worry potential as thoroughly as you have your digestive tract. Indigestion and the fear of insolvency may lead to only fitful sleep.

Royal Family

To express a worry about the Queen, although at the time it may not be altogether genuinely felt, shows that you are in essence a caring person. My late uncle was able to increase his worry potential over the years to such an extent that he was forced to dry his eyes whenever the late monarch but one appeared on the cinema screen. 'He looks, poor man, as if he desperately needs a holiday,' he would remark between his helpless sobs. Nowadays the customary rude health of the monarch and her family does not permit such sympathetic consideration but it is still possible to worry about the Prince of Wales finding a suitable bride, or even an unsuitable one. Those of us who were alive at the time remember how we worried about his great uncle being able to stay on a horse, before we realized that it was his throne that was destined to throw him.

An opportunity to meet with one of the family provides endless worry opportunities. What to wear, how to reply if one is actually spoken, to, how to keep one's balance in a curtsey, how to advance, retreat and, almost too frightening to contemplate, what to do in the event of collision. Suppose your petticoat fell down or your trousers, that you passed a rude noise, or, worse still, suddenly became incontinent, or experienced an uncontrollable impulse to stab her. Her Majesty has asked you to tea and despite your anxieties even the corgis seem to like you. The Queen instead of handing you a second cup places it on the floor and encourages you to lap it up. What to do? (The last is a dream you will worry about when you wake up. It could mean anything.)

School

Worries about school, implanted in children at an early age, will haunt them in various forms throughout life. Once they are instilled, the pupil will aways continue to measure what little skill he possesses and how successfully he deploys it against the achievements of others who originally outpaced him on the playing fields, and knocked him out of the boxing contest. Forever afterwards he will yearn in vain for favourable marks and a satisfactory report from his bank manager, his bishop if he goes into the church, or the plantation owner if he is a wage slave. Others will decide whether he is to be promoted or passed over, allowed to join the Diners Club or The Garrick and the exact sum to be paid to him annually as a leaving prize when he finally passes out. In his old age, he will be concerned with the obituarist's opinion of his merit.

The greatest service a parent can render a child is to throw school reports unread into the waste-paper basket and defy his son or daughter to fish them out and discover at their peril what has been written about them. Any success I have achieved on the stage has been due to my father's unflinching and inexplicable confidence and my own lack of curiosity at an early age. In later life I not only read but accumulated many volumes of press cuttings, but by then I was able to worry about other things. I do not need to remind readers of worries experienced in the chilling atmosphere of class and changing-rooms when they discovered that others learnt more easily, ate faster, went to the lavatory more regularly and managed to tie their shoe-laces. Some of these have disappeared, if only for the moment.

Sea

During the summer most people try to get as close to it as possible. There are attendant worries, such as the state of the tide, the com-parative size of the breakers, jellyfish, involuntary and sometimes permanent submersion, oil-slicks, sunburn, broken glass, sheer cliffs, how to undress and where (a rapidly disappearing worry, along with choice of swimming costume), objects which float out to sea and the occasional dead dog which floats in. In addition you can worry about pollution, the temperature and whether any or all of the members of your own family are at any given moment drowning.

For those who inexplicably choose to live permanently near the sea, there will be many a night when they will lie awake wondering if this time they will be engulfed or wake in the morning to discover a Japanese stone garden where the herbaceous border was the night before. During the summer they can worry about the constant demands of holiday-makers for toilet and telephone facilities and during the winter months that they will be blown out to sea along with the carport, or that one evening they will glimpse a distress rocket and forget to telephone the coast guards.

Sex

This provides, together with health and money to both of which it is closely linked, enormous opportunities throughout life. Whereas the sex life of the queen bee is over and done with before she can fly away, man's preoccupation starts in early childhood and persists into old age. Moreover, sexual activity enjoys the inestimable worry advantage of being, if not downright sinful, at least frowned upon by churches and their elders of all denominations. Movement of the bowels, OK. Movement of the loins, unless licensed by church or secular authority, very far from OK.

Sex is almost anything you wish it to be in the worry catalogue – an embarrassment, a health hazard, a skill to be perfected, a weapon to be wielded, a guilt to be concealed, something to deny yourself or others, a gift to be squandered, a commodity to be marketed, a trust to be betrayed. Sex can be a dirty postcard, a cane, a sauna, clothes on a washing line, a locked drawer, an address book, cash on the mantelpiece, a gentlemen's lavatory, a frantic exposure, the consummation of love, a peeping Tom. Only a few more general aspects for worry can be dealt with here, alas.

Sexual aberrations. A largely discarded worry. You are not, gentle reader, the only one who craves a Japanese midget dressed in chain-armour but if you wish to worry about this, please do so.

Sex symbols. Almost everything in sight, from the teapot to the arch-deacon's gaiters, and thus an almost permanent source of potential worry.

Sex change. The substitution of one love for another or a sophisti-cated game in which one of the players changes sides, often

permanently, after a small operation. Worries associated with the former circumstance include how to break the news, expense, danger of armed assault, when to call for the luggage, and have you done the right thing?

Kinks. How to explain to your new partner that you are at your best after paste sandwiches or while listening to a recording of 'When We Were Very Young' read by the late Donald Wolfit. In the latter case where do you shop around for your new image?

Sex education. Now taught in school classrooms as well as the customary site behind the gymnasium.

Sex discussion. Once a one-sided affair between schoolteacher and child, leading to increased mystification on the part of each. The subject is now under continuous discussion, particularly on the media, and is eagerly read and listened to by those who are hesitant to try or too old to perform the act themselves and prefer to worry from a safe distance.

Sexual fantasy. Anything from the plundering of Brigitte Bardot to the successful pursuit of a one-legged bus conductress, consummated on the stairway of a Number 11 bus hurtling along the Kings Road. This is simply fantastic, you may tell yourself, but the lurking worry that you may never achieve your ambition persists.

Sexual impotence. An ever-present fear and once realized, the subsequent post-mortem is an occasion for prolonged worry. What, you will ask yourself, went wrong? Your mother's photograph on the bedside table? The sudden onslaught of lumbago? Your partner's insistence on finishing a chapter or her prolonged tooth-brushing when you were all ready for the fray? Or was it one of those simple statements: 'You should have thought of it before I put my hair in curlers.' 'You don't mind if we cut out the foreplay, I have to be on court in ten minutes.' 'I don't think you quite understand the position. Why don't you have another look at the diagram?'

Sharks

A trip to the seaside has always been fraught with exciting worries but none so highly exhilarating as the notion that maybe today will be the day when, paddling off the rocks at Bournemouth, you will be eaten by a shark. Until Mr Benchley recognized the potential of the Great White, only life-guards on Bondi Beach worried about getting their legs nibbled. The arrival of films detailing, in glorious technicolour, the eating habits of these sneakily omnivorous creatures have made shark-worry both universal and fashionable. Sightings have even been reported in swimming pools, although investigation revealed only permanently circling cleaning apparatus. Do not, however, become so immersed in worrying about sharks that you neglect other possibilities presented to us over the years by the cinema, from man-eating plants to vampires, giant ants and werewolves.

Ships

A great deal of really pleasurable worry can be generated by a decision to avoid the worry of flying (*see* Aeroplanes) in favour of the sea. Anxiety starts when you try to come to grips with the early paperwork. The ticket or contract lists an alarming number of potentially disastrous circumstances in any or all of which the line is not responsible for compensation, even while you are on their premises. They not only indemnify themselves against any pecuniary loss you may incur by reason of shipwreck, mutiny and seizure of the vessel by armed pirates but also you are, or soon will be, honour bound to support the Captain against mutiny, to obey his slightest wish and, should you die during the voyage, to agree that he and he alone is the sole arbiter of what to do with your remains. Moreover, it is up to him to decide your eventual destination and should he decide against the Caribbean and continue to sail up and down the English Channel, you will not be permitted to storm the bridge and seize the steering wheel.

Most ships have now gone over to what is known as one-class accommodation thus depriving first-class passengers of the perpetual anxiety that a second- or even third-class passenger might leap the barriers and find a way through the service hatch to infiltrate their preserve. However, there are still two classes on board. One consists of the passengers and crew, and the other the Captain and just conceivably the First Officer.

Before stepping on board, you will do well to examine the ship's plan, after which you will be instantly worried by the realization that your cabin is not where you would have wished it to be. Perusal of the conditions set out in a brochure entitled 'Shipmates' and giving a list of the so-called amenities, such as bingo sessions and compulsory boat drill, will ensure further anxieties. If your departure is not at too distant a date you may also be provided with a passenger list. This is daunting in that it lists no one you have ever heard of except, of course, yourself and someone who may be, but almost certainly is not, the Astronomer Royal. Long before you are due to embark, you realize the whole venture is doomed, a feeling confirmed by the sight of your fellow passengers standing in long lines to await approval by customs and excise, health authorities, policemen, security guards, port officials and steamship representatives, watched by a sprinkling of amused and striking dockers and deck-hands.

Pinned in by officialdom and temporary steel barriers, you get your first glimpse of the discipline to which you must now submit for the next week or two.

Separated from your luggage, with which you are unlikely to be reunited for some time, you set off to find your cabin. After an exhausting process of trial and error you find it, only to realize that you are unlikely ever to do so again. Now is the time to test the light switches, satisfy yourself that your bunk is as hard and narrow as you expected it to be and read a card on the water jug which states that passenger luggage must be deposited outside the cabin by six o'clock previous to the day on which you intend to disembark. There is nothing to do but find the bar (closed), the library (closed), and the dining-room reservation desk, at which a small queue has already formed.

The question of table reservation is for most passengers a gnawing anxiety. It is up to the Purser to size you up or down and seat you where he considers you will enjoy the company and, less hopefully, the food, after which it is up to you to change the arrangement and spend the rest of the voyage being over-effusive and apologetic to your original table-mates. You will also have to lie to them and invent an imaginary old schoolfriend or the widow of your local chiropodist who has insisted, alas, that you join her table for the duration, though of course you would have infinitely preferred your original placement.

There are, luckily for the compulsive worrier, endless other opportunities for indulging his predilection while at sea. There is rough weather, ahead or being experienced, fear that the vessel may sink or lose her propellers, whether to ignore the summons to boat drill, how to capture a deck chair and where to place it, which side of the boat is port, and how to avoid having to share your cabin when more passengers come aboard at Cherbourg. Which shore excursion should you choose and when should you start to queue for the launch, the foreign exchange control, the buffet lunch round the swimming pool, the cinema and the Captain's cocktail party? Once ashore in foreign ports, how do you avoid getting robbed, or arrested by secret police? There is the ever-present anxiety that you may miss the bus after the visit to the Botanical Gardens and, of course, the boat also. Finally, towards the end of the voyage, how can you avoid giving your address to various acquaintances and should you declare the alleged gold bracelet you bought in the souk along with the carpet? And how much it is going to cost to replace the lost movie camera your bank manager insisted on lending you, along with the money you have just spent?

Sleep

There are a great many ways to avoid worry over the lack of this, medical prescriptions being the most favoured. Confirmed insomniacs, such as the late Charles Boyer, tend to regard an inability to sleep as a minor inconvenience. It is the occasional sleepless night of the regular sleeper that really bites. If I didn't sleep last night, how do I know I shall sleep tonight? You probably won't. On the other hand, tomorrow night you should be so thoroughly tired that you will almost certainly drop off. Does it matter, not sleeping? It isn't as if you get a respite from activity. Everyone thrashes about and the brain positively races. Some think the heartbeats slow down but surely that it the last thing to be desired – they might stop altogether. I cannot therefore conscientiously recommend this worry. When a man informs me that he was so worried he couldn't sleep a wink I cannot commiserate. He is attempting to do two things which cannot be performed simultaneously. Aren't you forgetting nightmares, you ask, or don't you worry during your own? Like most actors I dream sometimes I hear the cue for my entrance on stage and for some reason cannot gain access to it, or that I am standing in front of the footlights already costumed and made up for a role of which I do not remember one word. But a nightmare is an entirely different

'What do you mean – it's fitted with a silencer?'

worry from insomnia. You have to have stopped worrying about not being able to sleep before you can have a nightmare.

Falling asleep involuntarily is the reverse side of the coin. As life continues, the ability to drop off to sleep is a skill many would like to discard. They worry lest a quick nap at the wheel could be indefinitely prolonged. In theatres and when watching television it becomes increasingly difficult to follow the action, and friends and relatives tend to look askance at the sleeper, his head swivelled forward and a rhythmic wheezing proceeding from his slackened mouth. How sad to reflect that when he dozed as a babe people smiled happily and spoke in whispers. On the whole I prefer not to wake a friend who falls asleep while I am talking to him. I worry lest his remorse should be too great for him to bear.

Speeches

Just a few words. Yes, but which? Why did I agree to go to the dinner in the first place? I shan't be able to eat or drink. Dare I leave it to the spur of the moment? Chuck it at the last minute? Simply send a greetings telegram apologizing for a head cold? How long do they expect me to go on and about what for heavens sake? What sort of idiots are they who are willing to pay seven guineas for a ticket? At least they won't expect me to pay, or will they? Of course not, I am singing for my supper.

'I realize that to sing for one's supper demands a voice truer than my own. But I felt I simply had to come here this evening to propose the toast of the guests and particularly Mrs Blenkinsop, the well-known ex-prison governor.' (That's what they say she did.) 'I only hope there won't be a riot here this evening.' That would put the cat among the pigeons, but I suppose it's a no-go area. Cat among the pigeons? 'I feel like a cat among' ... or better, perhaps, 'We all feel we are pigeons flocking to welcome the cat.' Hopeless. Better to leave Mrs B out altogether than insult the poor woman. How about, 'I must confess I felt a bit redundant introducing Mrs Blenkinsop. Some of you might have met her already under less happy circumstances.' It might get a laugh unless there were a couple of ex-gaolbirds sopping up the gravy. Gravy? Porridge? Surely that's safe. 'I half expected in view of Mrs Blenkinsop's presence that we might start with porridge rather than grapefruit.' Better perhaps not to try and be too witty. Once I get a reputation for this sort of thing I might have to do it again. How about, 'Ladies and Gentlemen, my brief is to introduce our guests, handcuffed to the name of the principal speaker Mrs Blenkinsop.' People don't like long speeches. 'Mrs Blenkinsop must by this time be used to captive audiences but I suggest to you that this is the first time . . .' for what in heaven's name? Concentrate. How long have I got? Where's the calendar. Another month?

'For the last month, ever since I knew I was speaking this evening, I have felt like a condemned criminal marking off the hours until his execution.' A shade sombre. I wonder if Mrs Blenkinsop has ever seen an execution? Shall I tell them that when I agreed to make a speech I thought I'd think of something to say but I never did, then just sit down and hope to get into the Guinness Book of Records? There must be more important things to worry about; it's just that at this moment I can't think of them. If I were to be wrecked on a desert island with six gramophone records but without Mr Roy Plumley, what single object would I most like to take with me? The notes for my speech welcoming Mrs Blenkinsop to the Rotarian Guest Night dinner which circumstances beyond my control prevented me from delivering, to remind me how lucky I have always been – up to now at any rate.

Stars

There are occasional anxious moments connected with the firmament when I worry whether the Astronomer Royal has not got it right after all and at any moment the whole thing may fall down on top of me. The moon herself seems to delight in playing tricks; quite often I have remarked that she is extraordinarily low in the heavens and appears to be out of control and falling rapidly.

When Mr Armstrong first stepped on to the moon's surface I held my breath. 'The idiot,' I told myself, 'is in for a surprise.' I don't say I worried too much – I didn't even know him – nor was it (except for a small part of my film residuals) my money they were spending on his fare. But I do worry about the way things are going. We are all apparently travelling at an immense speed. Common sense urges that one day (though not, I trust, in my lifetime) we shall arrive somewhere we don't wish to be. Meanwhile, having been born under Gemini, I read the horoscopes available to me in the media. Only this morning I learnt that it would be better for me to stay put all day as moving from place to place will be a very slow process and a disappointing one at that. My energy is likely to be heavily drained and companions apt to be moody. I am warned not to upset them. Tomorrow I am to expect a complete change of atmosphere: companions will now be in exuberant spirits and it won't be long before I too am in a happy-go-lucky mood. I beg leave, however, to doubt this. The long-term forecast is threatening. Venus is about to join forces with Uranus and this augurs poorly for financial stability; I am exhorted to redouble my efforts and prepare for a major disappointment.

I am not fond of barking up the wrong tree. If this book isn't going to sell, I would be grateful for more specific pronouncements. On the other hand, the final prognostication affords a crumb of comfort: if trying to raise funds via loans, the outlook is more promising, particularly if I am willing to go to extra expense by putting in long-distance phone calls. But then again to whom exactly? It's all very worrying.

Swimming Pools

One of the great summer worries. Construction can also cause anxiety (*see* Builders) but once the pool is operational you will become your own maintenance man. A great deal can go wrong in a pool besides drowning. One does not just bathe in water but a delicate combination of chemical additives, and to obtain the correct mix is a highly-skilled operation. Fear that a pool may suddenly lose its crystalline and desirable appearance and become opaque and socially unacceptable causes many a sleepless night and dawn visits to the waterside.

While the hot spell is quiescent, the question of heating the pool or not heating it can be mulled over, along with the considerable expense involved. If the former course of action is adopted it must be set against the worry that having heated the water no one will want to bathe after all. Removing leaves and beetles from the surface and band aids from the bottom along with goggles and flippers may not be a worry in itself but this and other time-consuming tasks, such as seeing what can be done about leaks (nothing), may cause the owner to brood on the advisability of filling in the damn thing next autumn and trying for asparagus.

Weekends are worry peaks. 'The kids are a bit bored, can I bring them to swim? Just rang up to ask what sort of temperature you are maintaining? We have some Frenchies staying, we've told them about your pool. You mean Rupert is down there on his own? Keep an eye on Guy, he is a frightfully keen little fellow simply doesn't know what fear is. I thought if you threw them in when they were two years old, they knew instinctively how to float. Sylvia wants to try giving you the kiss of life.'

Teeth

Tooth worry is sometimes triggered by pain, when it is usually of a temporary nature and may subside after a visit to the dentist. If of this kind, you could follow Huw Wheldon's maxim: 'A toothache can often be cured by laying out a few old copies of *Punch* on your own dining-table.' Much more lasting is a widely-held anxiety that all your teeth may one day fall out, or splinter into small fragments which should on no account be swallowed. Just as some may never learn to walk on crutches, one cannot help but observe the trouble others have with dentures. For this reason many people grow morbidly attached to their own teeth and find themselves worrying over them to the point when they no longer willingly engage in fights or eat Brighton rock. Towards old age this obsessive sense of possession becomes increasingly articulate and octogenarians take a pride in announcing that their teeth are their own, even if, as is so often not the case with the rest of us, they haven't had to pay a penny for them. Worrying about other people's teeth, especially when they flash on the television screen, is fairly common.

When a child loses his milk teeth nature replaces them but when he loses the last of the second lot, he is back to milk (Chinese Proverb).

Telephones

It is possible to worry from time to time about other household appliances – the toaster, the dishwasher, the spin-drier all have off days – but the telephone alerts even when it is most silent. Why is it not ringing, we ask ourselves? It is highly unlikely, surely, that our loved one, who had promised to telephone the moment she arrived home, having consulted her mother about the day for our wedding, has forgotten the whole plan. She is either dead in a ditch or, more probably, her mother has countermanded the engagement.

On the other hand, whenever the telephone does ring, we ask ourselves why. Possibilities of disaster crowd in upon us. The mere act of answering the bell may lead to disaster. A rug slips in our unseemly haste to get the receiver off the hook and a fresh call for an ambulance becomes necessary. Even more worrying is to encounter silence or heavy breathing at the end of the wire. This could mean anything – a burglar on his way, if not this evening at least later in the week, or a killer on the loose who has finally tracked down his next victim and will shortly be calling in person. It is only prudent to try making a call of your own after a few minutes. If the phone has now gone dead you are, whether you like it or not, in Hitchcock country and must decide whether to make a dash for it or see that all windows and doors are secure.

My own worry when making a phone call has been greatly increased by the STD system which, by the sheer weight of the numbers involved, makes it impossible to retain them in anything like the right order once I have shut the book. In seeking the operator's by no means ready help, I have not only added to the cost of the call but demonstrated yet again my personal inadequacy. In the event of there being no reply, it is vain to argue with authority that there is a baby somewhere in the house so there must also be a mother, or that you happen to know your friend is bedridden and the instrument always within reach. Perhaps the most sinister of all replies is the one about

the service having been discontinued. This can only mean that the invalid is now penniless and the baby starving.

A telephone provides infinite opportunity for the compulsive worrier, not the least of which will be the telephone bill when it arrives. There is also the anxiety to be experienced once you decide to enter a public call-box from which the phone has already been removed or, at best, is out of order. While you are considering your next move, you will encounter furious tapping on the door by someone who quite obviously is only waiting for you to emerge so that he can relieve you of your handbag or wallet. In the unlikely event of the phone being in working order, there is now the probability that the coin slot is jammed or that you have dropped all your available ten-pence pieces on the floor. How is it, you may ask yourself, that Doctor Who has made a happy and presumably profitable livelihood by shacking up in a police booth all these years? But then, if there is one thing *he* never does, it is worry.

Tourniquets

Can you apply one? Consider the circumstances in which you may have to.

Toys

Should a toy be 'educational' or not? And does rounding the edges of a bit of wood and neglecting to paint it really inspire the child to imaginative flights of fancy more than the tinny, wind-up clown that bangs a drum? One of the most successful toys introduced to our household was a mechanical fish which, when let loose, gobbled up a smaller fish. Does the delighted childish (and indeed adult) response to this indicate an underlying aggressive tendency? A toy store and a Christmas list can reduce the most decisive personality to dithers. It is a sobering thought that a momentary lapse in buying a junior chemistry set for that brilliant but hostile nephew could result in the destruction of three mock-Tudor houses in Tunbridge Wells.

Then there are children who so worry about breaking toys that they leave them in their wrappings to hand onto their own children. There are other children who worry if a toy remains unbroken on Boxing Day. They envisage a lifetime of boredom watching the indestructible train carrying on ceaselessly round the circular track. The greatest worry, however, is that box of slightly broken toys. They aren't bad enough to throw out but demand hours of skill to put back into working order.

Trains

This worry starts with the timetable. You cannot look up the connection too often or make sure that you made no mistake about the day of the week, month of the year, and whether you do or do not have to change at Cheltenham. Perhaps the best plan is to ring passenger enquiries when you have a free morning. No doubt you will want to arrive at the station in good time, to give yourself plenty of enjoyable worry about what happened to porters, and how to get your case on to the courtesy trolley, if you can find one, and up and down the stairs. A quarter of an hour after the taxi was due to arrive at your door is always a prime worry time.

The station gained, there are anxious minutes ahead of you while you wait in the ticket queue. The days when tickets were printed, ready and waiting, have disappeared, along with most of the booking clerks. There is seldom more than one window open and most of the other passengers will be paying by credit card or travelling on

mysterious rebate concessions. The paperwork involved is considerable and the delays mount up as those in front search pockets for
birth certificates, proof of identity and credit worthiness. Temptation to hasten the proceedings by announcing you have a train to
catch will be disregarded while the complexity and cost of the travel
plans of a single parent taking advantage of the concessions available
to her for spending two nights and a day in Colwyn Bay and
travelling with three children – one free, one carried and the third
in charge of her aged grandmother (more concessions available here)
– are estimated, finally agreed and charged to her building society
insurance account.

The public address system, besides announcing inaudibly at which
platform your train is now standing, is concerned with a number of
extraneous and potentially worrying matters. Why, for instance,
should a Mrs Carstairs meeting her daughter off the train from
Wolverhampton be urged to contact the station master? A number
of horrendous possibilities must present themselves to a caring
person. Did her daughter meet with a fatal accident before even taking
her seat in the train? No, that would have allowed time for Mrs
Carstairs to be contacted. Something must have occurred after the
train left Wolverhampton and while Mrs Carstairs's daughter was
incommunicado. But what? Has there been a crash on the line? But
in that case surely all passengers, friends and relatives would have
been alerted. She fell out of the window, perhaps, or on to the track
just after the engine gathered speed and it has taken time,
naturally, before she could be identified. You will probably never
know the truth of this one, any more than you will be able to fathom
the reason why the St John's Ambulance Corps attendant is required
urgently in the parcels office, but it is something to think about as
you sit in your carriage pondering why the train has not left on time
and whether the youth fast asleep opposite is suffering from some
tropical fever of a particularly virulent variety or has merely been
rendered insensible by a drug problem. When, after a further delay,
the train is still standing motionless, you may begin to ask yourself
whether it is indeed the one you imagined it to be, or could the train

now pulling out of the station on another line be the one you should be on for Ledbury?

Just as you lean out of the window seeking a fellow traveller or some minor official to reassure yourself that you will eventually be deposited where you were hoping, the train will suddenly pull away. Besides the worry that you are now steaming rapidly in the wrong direction is added the doubt about whether you remembered your sponge bag. Did you leave it on the lavatory seat? By now you are pretty certain you did just that. You are getting more and more concerned about increasing forgetfulness and about your companion, whose hideous pallor and incomprehensible muttering make you look around for the exact location of the communication cord.

For the compulsive travel worrier, I do not need to suggest further anxieties that you will enjoy on your journey. You will have an ample supply on which to draw, from wondering whether in fact the train was passing a station when you decided to pull the plug, to whether the youth you left asleep is now staggering along the platform under the after-effects of pot and the weight of his newly-acquired luggage. By now you will have been reassured that you are indeed destined to alight at Ledbury but that, as the train is exactly an hour and a half late, you will miss the memorial service.

Visiting

Unless I am at a loss for something to worry about, I seldom these days accept invitations to stay with friends, although I sometimes worry about how rarely I am asked to do so. Years ago I jumped at the chance of getting away from enforced frugality and mixing with the landed gentry. Kent was a favourite stomping ground, particularly one moated grange whose owner kept all manner of servants including Mesmer, her chauffeur. Chauffeurs are a lively source of worry to their employers at all times and Mesmer was no exception. Although a younger and steadier hand at the wheel might have been thought desirable, our hostess's loyalty to her ex-gardener remained unbounded. 'I simply don't know what I should do without him,' she was wont to remark, but with the passing of time I detected an increasing lack of confidence on her part in his ability to perform his functions. My own confidence in Mesmer suffered no such decline. I never had any, and as we swerved and bucked along the leafy lanes, I never needed to remind myself that Mesmer had never had to pass the test. At least, when I left it was not necessary to be lavish with the tip. Driving as Mesmer did, he might easily not survive till my next visit.

Water

Being a basic human need, water is an excellent source of worry. The French worry about drinking the water in Italy, Germans worry about drinking the water in France, the British worry about drinking the water 'abroad' and Americans worry about drinking the water from any tap at all. Should water have fluoride injected into it? What else are 'they' putting into our water? Besides the actual state of the water, it is also possible to worry about too much water, too little water, frozen water, water-pipes, water on the knee and hydrophobia (*see also* Sharks).

Weather

Although a few people are paid to worry about the weather and even to appear nightly on television to inform us of the awful times ahead caused by the arrival of the customary depression off our coasts, most carry out the task on an unpaid if no less enthusiastic basis.

Like a daily newspaper, the weather provides fresh anxiety each morning. Even when an occasional dry spell occurs, we begin to worry about emptied reservoirs and how to transfer the rationed bath water to the rose beds.

Normally in Britain there is always the threat of rain to bring sleepless hours to those in charge of organizing the village fête. Others, perched uneasily on the seat of government, have even graver responsibility in these matters. When should they open the sluice gates on the Thames, or hurry sandbags to Deal?

The worry of whether to set forth with umbrella or sunshade is a symptom of much deeper anxieties. Tomorrow, perhaps, the flood – or the return of the ice age. Will polar bears be seen again in Orpington, or our great-great-grandchildren fail to adapt to the utterly changed environment and simply disappear overnight from the Isle of Wight, as did the great auk in his day? Yet it is only when the weather decides never to change that we shall all have to worry in earnest.

Wills

Not being able to take it with you is often a cause of worry for the comparatively careful spender and for those who have spent a lifetime accumulating a collection of postage stamps or coins in the bank. Hence the phrase 'last will and testament' is something to be carefully considered by all concerned. A will is a worry for those who hope to share the legacies but how much more pleasurable an anxiety it is for those who won't be there when it's read. 'To my nephew who, I regretfully must now place on record, has never had the slightest knowledge of the meaning of money, I bequeath the sum of fifty pounds annually, to be paid in half-yearly instalments, as long as he shall be in what the trustees may decide is meaningful employment

and has remained so without resource to public funds or anticipation of any benefit he may receive from claims on my estates during the last ten years. In the event that he becomes a public servant such as a fireman or road-mender, park-keeper or dustman, whole or part-time, he forfeits all future claims to benefit, as I am convinced, were he so to do, the community would be at risk.'

A certain amount of worrying over the wording of a will ensures that the actual document will be almost impossible to fathom in the final draft. Setting the legatees conundrums associated with vulgar fractions, participatory life interests, reversions and entailment of interest due on the death of a remote cousin who disappeared into the Australian bush many years before, can add enormously to the worry mountain you hope to create. Some solicitors insert a clause expressly forbidding the contesting of a will on forfeiture of the litigant's right to benefit under it. This invariably leads to further fruitful anxiety.

Some worry lest the mere act of making a will will hasten their own demise. Readers are urged to dismiss this theory from their minds and set about consulting a suitable solicitor as soon as possible. Once the will is drawn up, it can be altered by codicils and leaked at your discretion, providing infinite worry for all. Remember that every time you send for your solicitors, your relatives and companions will hasten to rearrange your pillows.

Zoos

The hastily-made and usually ill-considered promise made to the
children (any children) of an outing to the zoo produces a myriad
of worries (over and above the likelihood of losing them there) as
the appointed day approaches. Who first thought of rounding up
animals, transporting them across continents and oceans at great
expense, not to mention danger (to all concerned) and putting them
behind bars? I would never, sitting by the fireside, have thought:
'Wouldn't it be nice to catch a tiger and bring it home for the
children to see' – and I am well known for original thinking. What
kind of mind formulated the concept of zoos and did it ever worry,
having accomplished it, what worries it would bestow on the animals
and the rest of us? Do the animals worry about being looked at
or not being looked at sufficiently? Or do they worry about us, lined
up outside the cage. 'Here's ole Harry again,' the chimpanzee says
to his mate. 'Brought the grandchildren today, I see. Think he's looking tired, don't you?'

How are you ever going to explain to the children that you have
no intention of putting five pence into the machine that dispenses
strawish, peanutty substances with which (and only which) you are
allowed to feed the animals, because you worry about how to explain

the loss of digits to the other relatives? There is also the ever-present worry that one of your charges, like Albert, will slip under the bars and be devoured by a lion. Safari Parks have been as much a boon to mankind as zoos, so many worries do they excite.

So wind up the windows and lock the doors tight
Remember my son that a monkey can bite.
Though the beasts of the jungle are all at large
His Grace is the only one able to charge.

compiled and edited by Robert Morley
illustrated by Geoffrey Dickinson and John Jensen
Robert Morley's Book of Bricks £1.25

The hilarious, best-selling collection of things people say – and then
wish they hadn't . . .

'Whatever happened to that skinny blonde your husband was once
married to?'
'I dyed my hair,' replied the lady.

A whole concert of clangers culled from everyone who will admit to
brick-dropping.

All royalties donated to the National Society for Autistic Children.

Rob Buckman
Out of Practice 95p

Do you need a course of yellow fever injections to enter a Chinese
restaurant? Did your father ever strip naked, do handsprings against
the bathroom door while shrieking out French irregular verbs? No?
Between the covers of this book lurk the innermost thoughts and crazy
experiences of a practising medic – the only man to invent a cure for
which there is no known disease. Illustrated by Bill Tidy, this hilarious
book's author is still a practising registrar in a London hospital.

'The funniest thing to come out of a hospital since Richard Gordon'
SHERIDAN MORLEY

You can buy these and other Pan books from booksellers and
newsagents; or direct from the following address:
Pan Books, Sales Office, Cavaye Place, London SW10 9PG
Send purchase price plus 20p for the first book and 10p for
each additional book, to allow for postage and packing
Prices quoted are applicable in the UK

While every effort is made to keep prices low, it is sometimes
necessary to increase prices at short notice. Pan Books reserve
the right to show on covers and charge new retail prices which
may differ from those advertised in the text or elsewhere